Writing Recommendation Letters
The Discourse of Evaluation in
Academic Settings

Writing Recommendation Letters
The Discourse of Evaluation in Academic Settings

MOHAMMED ALBAKRY
AND CLINT BRYAN

University of Michigan Press
Ann Arbor

ISBN 978-0-472-03965-4 (print)
ISBN 978-0-472-22166-0 (e-book)

Contents

List of Tables and Figures ————————

Acknowledgments

This book (the first in a planned two volumes on evaluative discourse in academic settings) took many years to research and write. In the process, it has passed through several incarnations and stages of transformation. The results reflect our complementary strengths in linguistic and rhetorical analyses. Each of us worked on every section independently and collaboratively; we have no doubt that the collaboration has resulted in a far better scholarly work than either of us would have produced on our own.

We cannot possibly thank here all the many individuals who have supported us throughout the process of writing this book, but we are deeply grateful to all the many colleagues and administrators who generously shared their advice and responded to our questions. Mohammed Albakry would like to express his gratitude to Sharon Harris, former director of the University of Connecticut's Humanities Institute (UCHI), for her support of this project when it was still a nascent idea. He is also grateful for the support of the following colleagues: Jennifer Francois, Madonna Kemp, Viviana Cortes, and Eniko Csomay. For their institutional support of his research, he would like to thank Stephen Severn, chair of the Department of English at Middle Tennessee State University, and Rhonda McDaniel, director of Graduate Studies there. Clint Bryan would like to express his thanks to Sarah Drivdahl, provost of Northwest University, and to the faculty of the College of Arts and Sciences past and present, especially Renee Bourdeaux, Traci Grant, Chrystal Helmcke, Will Mari, Joe McQueen, Lenae Nofziger, Jacob Witt, and Jeremiah Webster. Both authors would also like to thank Katie LaPlant, associate editor at University of Michigan Press, for believing in this project and providing great support and valuable feedback as the work progressed. Finally, and most importantly, we would like to express our gratitude to our families for their endless support and encouragement: Judy Albakry; Sami Albakry; Amanda Albakry; Sally Bryan; Cori Latcham; and Tyler and Abby Stovall.

Introduction

General Overview

"Language is the most massive and inclusive art we know, a mountainous and anonymous work of unconscious generations."
  —Edward Sapir, *Language: An Introduction to the Study of Speech*

While it is true that language can be the most inclusive art we know, it can also be exclusive. Some discourse types are not equally available or accessible to everyone except for the privileged few. Such is the case with reference letters, otherwise known as letters of recommendation (henceforward LORs) in academic circles. If you choose to embark on a career teaching in any higher education setting, from a local community college or vocational school to a prestigious R1 university, you will be required to write LORs for any number of scenarios. Call it something of an occupational hazard because the requests seem to come at the busiest times in the semester. The problem, however, is that most academics have never been formally taught the inherent moves within a successful LOR written for a given occasion. Instead, many novice faculty members have had to teach themselves how to write these genres by picking up the linguistic and rhetorical conventions as they go along. It is unsurprising, then, why many of us in academe remain in the dark about this ever-present formal genre.

Like peer-review writing, the LOR genre is taken for granted and hardly ever taught. Graduate students in professional development seminars or workshops are trained in crafting CVs and cover letters, as well as giving job talks and conference presentations, among other career-preparation skills. However, they often are not advised on how to read and write thoughtful and informative recommendation letters. Unlike dissertations or research papers that enjoy wider exposure, LORs often lack public presence and thus can be described as an occluded, or "behind-the-scenes," institutional genre, i.e., "out of sight to outsiders and apprentices" (Swales, 2004, p. 18; see also Feak, 2009; Swales, 1996). They have also been called "support" or "supporting" genres (Swales, 2004; Swales & Feak, 2011), a term that we prefer to use in this book.

In any case, due to confidentiality concerns, LORs tend to be hidden from the public gaze, but they still underpin the academic administrative processes of admission, hiring, or securing grants and fellowships, and can be crucial factor in determining who may be granted a job interview, a coveted fellowship, or tenure and promotion. Therefore, it is important to know how to write successful academic LORs, the underlying purpose of the content and activities embedded in this book.

Drawing on close to a thousand LORs, this book aims to shed light on the linguistic features, rhetorical conventions, and discursive strategies of these important evaluative text types. The texts comprising the corpus are drawn mostly from the diverse fields of the humanities and social sciences (e.g., history, anthropology, medieval studies, linguistics, literature, sociology, classics, philosophy, rhetoric and composition, area studies, etc.) as well as education. Overall, the majority of the collected LOR samples fall into three categories defined by purpose: letters written for graduate admission, letters written in support of fellowship applications, and letters written to support obtaining a faculty position.

By analyzing letters from different academic areas, we provide a multi-perspective view of genres and genre study, thereby widening our understanding of the genre conventions. The findings have implications for genre-based writing instruction, English for Academic Purposes (EAP), and teaching of academic literacies. This theoretically grounded but practical book will thus be of great use to junior faculty who have managed to land academic jobs as well for those who hope to join the academy and its inhabitants. The real-world examples and authentic excerpts therein will also be of great benefit to graduate students and ABDs—all but dissertation students—who are just starting their academic careers, especially in the North American context. However, because of English globalization and the spread of the American model of education, we believe that users and instructors outside the United States will also benefit from the materials and analysis provided here.

Some remarks on the structure and our choice of terms and pronouns in the following chapters are in order. First, we use the terms "academy" and its different variations "academia" and "academe" interchangeably to refer to institutions of postsecondary education and higher learning. These institutions often perceive part of their mission as being agents of knowledge production and transmission. Regardless of their different academic disciplines, the faculty working in these academic institutions engage in teaching and pursuing scholarly research and writing.

Secondly, identifying features of personal identity were redacted from the majority of the letters collected in our corpus, and, therefore, gender was not a variable we investigated. We changed all pronouns to singular "they" (unless the gender distinction was clear and deemed germane to the narrative). In any case, we personally prefer to use singular "they" or "their" as a more gender-neutral pronoun option in place of the awkward "he or she" or "his and her." We are aware that some language purists may consider this usage grammatically incorrect, but prescriptive attitudes can and should change if they clash with appropriateness and inclusivity. We are in good company; *Merriam-Webster Dictionary* acknowledged the legitimacy of "singular they" in 2019, the same year as the *Publication Manual of the American Psychological Association* (APA), whose citation style is adopted in this book.

Thirdly, for the sake of pedagogical engagement, we round out most chapters with some discussion questions to invite readers to reflect deeply upon the implications of the respective genre and discussion presented in the chapter. We also provide tasks and brief sections that focus on interesting rhetorical and linguistic points emerging from the discussion. Of course, an instructor of a class in Writing in the Academy could assign one of the questions for a brief reflection or incorporate two or three in classroom discussions of a given subtype of LORs. While the intended audience for these questions may be graduate students enrolled in a course on academic writing or junior faculty embarking on a series of "firsts" in their academic careers (e.g., writing a first letter of recommendation for a colleague's fellowship application), the seasoned professor also stands to benefit from contemplating these topics further. If we hope to remain agile in the shifting employment and scholarly landscape, we do well to stay abreast of the best practices emerging from real-world research, as demonstrated in this book.

Finally, while we seek to define key terms as they arise in the subsequent chapters, the glossary at the conclusion of this volume elaborates on some of the major concepts and will prove helpful for becoming familiar with the salient terms used in the study.

Impetus for the Book

This is the first volume of a planned two-book sequence on the language of evaluative discourse in the academic context; the discourse of recommendation letters is the focus in this volume, while the upcoming volume covers the different statements of job applications, such as the research statement (RS); the teaching philosophy statement (TPS); and the diversity, equity, and inclusion statement (DEI). It may be helpful to think of both volumes as building upon the strong foundation laid by genre studies pioneers John Swales and Christine Feak more than a decade ago. In many ways, they work in tandem with their earlier publications.

The books build on the four titles in the *English in Today's Research World* collection, published by the University of Michigan Press in the English for Academic and Professional Purposes series (2009, 2011). These instructive textbooks helped to translate academic discursive practices into accessible language, supplying ample writing practice to those assigned to read them in graduate school. In turn, they helped thousands of nascent academics find their voice, particularly novice faculty and those for whom English is an additional language.

However, the most recent two books in this series are now twelve years old. As in any professional field, new advancements have continued in the ensuing years—changes that we try to cover in understandable language with plenty of practice. For instance, our second volume includes practice in writing the diversity, equity, and inclusion statement, a relative newcomer that emerged as a job application requirement in the intervening time since 2011. Because we translate recent corpus-based research into ways that graduate students and junior faculty in the humanities, education, and social sciences may apply to writing recommendation letters—an ongoing task for any academic—we recognize the debt that we owe to this successful first series and extend its impact by taking a deeper dive into other academic support genres.

The Research behind This Book

The guidelines and examples in this book are based on a specialized corpus of representative texts. Given the understandable confidentiality around which admission, hiring, and promotion operates within higher education, gathering the full data set proved challenging at times and took several years, including long delays to ensure that any identifiable features were obscured. Obtaining access to some of these confidential genres required repeated requests and assurances that the data would be used for research purposes only.

For the purpose of this study, we collected 815 authentic recommendation letters written for more than 300 individuals applying for nineteen assistant professor positions and two humanities fellowships at a diverse range of American universities. The letters encompass diverse fields within the humanities, social sciences, and education. Additionally, we also collected 160 letters submitted in support of admission to PhD granting graduate programs in English.

Despite its corpus-based approach and use of some quantification and descriptive statistics, the methodology of the study is fundamentally qualitative and interpretive. Our approach, for example, does not attempt to quantifiably measure variables or examine potential relationships between them. Rather than big-data and large corpora, the study is based on a "bespoke," specialized corpus of representative texts. However, our data set is large enough to be interrogated for frequency distribution of recurrent words and phrases, keywords, and collocations, with the added advantage of being more analytically amenable to close reading and detailed examination.

It is important to note, given the occluded nature of the LOR genre, that having large amounts of data sufficient for certain corpus techniques and statistical analyses is difficult. Consequently, our corpus may seem relatively small compared to other recent mixed-methods or quantitative analyses within genre discourse studies of publicly available texts such as journal article abstracts or conference proceedings (see Omidian et al., 2018). The structured set of texts comprising our data, however, is representative of an elusive genre that is notoriously difficult to collect because of its private nature. By using purposeful sampling and segmenting the corpus into distinct sub-corpora and, at times, analyzing each sub-corpus individually for its distinct rhetorical and linguistic features, we are able to give a clearer picture of different specific types of recommendation in this academic macrogenre.

Corpus- and genre-based approaches serve as the general analytic framework for this study. The corpus-based linguistic approach provides an empirical, methodical (bottom-up) inquiry into the textual patterns and lexico-grammatical features, while the Swalesian genre-based approach explores through a top-down analysis the shared conventions of rhetorical composition of texts. These analytical approaches complement each other in exploring the range of linguistic choices and rhetorical options by combining both "functional-qualitative" methods with corpus-based, quantitative processes that allow the findings to be interpreted accurately

(Biber et al., 2007, p. 241). You will encounter real-world examples drawn from actual LORs to see how seasoned faculty frame certain ideas to build their case for the applicants in question. The opinions of faculty and administrators sprinkled throughout many chapters should also give you a glimpse into the attitudes toward and assessments of different strategies in the evaluative discourse of LORs.

The Outline of the Book

Besides the general overview and conclusion, the book is divided into seven chapters. The first chapter provides the necessary theoretical context for studying occluded and academic support genres, paying special attention to the major principles of defining genre, particularly the private genre of recommendation letters. Chapter two dives into the varied purposes of recommendation letters by breaking the LOR genre down into three different types (highlighting similarities and differences when relevant) according to specific purposes: 1.) LORs written for graduate doctoral admission; 2.) LORs written for postdoctoral research fellowships; and 3.) LORs written for academic job applications. The chapter also tackles the notion of positioning oneself as a recommender as well as the overall role of recommendation letters in the academic setting. The remaining chapters focus on different aspects of the linguistic and rhetorical features of recommendation discourse in areas such as presenting the applicants' credentials, highlighting the strengths of their character, accentuating and downplaying certain traits, as well as the pros and cons of boilerplate language and the use of customary frames for opening and closing.

Reading and writing recommendation letters is one of the essential service tasks of the professorial life of academics. May this theoretically informed but practice-oriented book help you feel better prepared to write your first (or your fiftieth) academic recommendation letter.

CHAPTER 1

Occluded (Support) Genres

Overview

Genre studies, as the word "studies" implies, is an interdisciplinary academic field devoted to research into analyzing texts in terms of conventions, styles, and constraints that guide the processes of their production and interpretation. Different scholars operating in the field of academic and professional genre analysis (i.e., non-literary genres), however, have different interests and goals, but, in general, they can be divided into two broad camps: the linguistic camp and the rhetorical camp. While the following discussion can sound a little technical, it is nonetheless helpful to realize that language researchers who set out to study particular genres have come from different theoretical perspectives.

The researchers in the first camp often take a text-linguistic perspective influenced by the Hallidayan approach of Systemic Functional Linguistics (SFL) and its view of language as a social semiotic system and language structure as part of a text's context and function. They are also often interested in examining the pedagogical implications of their research for language learning and teaching—especially in English for Specific Purposes (ESP) and English for Professional Academic Purposes (EPAP) (see Belcher et al., 2016).

Scholars in the rhetorical camp, on the other hand, have traditionally seemed more interested in genre analysis of the rhetorical macrostructures. They view genre and its textual features as traces of recurring social actions (Miller, 1984) and developing theories surrounding the social construction of reality (Christie & Martin, 2000). Carolyn Miller's supposition that "a genre is not just a pattern of forms" (1984, p. 165) complicates the notion that rhetorical genre studies (RGS) focuses exclusively on rhetorical figures and devices or various appeals to audience; nevertheless, some RGS scholars have begun to interrogate meso- and micro-level linguistic resources within a corpus for clues on how the various authors compose (Aull, 2015). It is now widely recognized that related text types combine to perform a given rhetorical purpose, and thus they can all belong to a "genre set," the accepted term for a particular constellation of genres "that enable particular groups of individuals to accomplish particular actions within a genre system" (Bawarshi, 2010, p. 88).

The distinction between applied linguistics and rhetorical studies is important for offering a starting point of comparison of LORs, but the dichotomy, if pressed too far, becomes artificial. Rather than a binary opposition of two competing approaches, however, other overviews of the major theoretical approaches to genre (e.g., Hyland, 2004b, 2004c; Hyon, 1996) tend to conceptualize the division as three broad perspectives including Systemic Functional Linguistics (Halliday & Martin, 1993)—genre as social purpose; New Rhetoric (Bazerman, 1988)—genre as situated action; and English for Specific Purposes (Swales, 1990)—genre as professional competence.

In his ground-breaking book, *Genre Analysis: English in Academic and Research Settings*, John Swales (1990) laid out the methodological approach that brought ESP and genre analysis together by emphasizing the commonalities between linguistic and rhetorical studies, thus paving the way for more cross-disciplinary collaboration for other studies like this one. He identified two characteristics of ESP genre analysis: its focus on academic research in English and its use for pedagogy and genre-based instruction—two considerations that reinforce our approach. Informed by the Swalesian model, our genre analysis embraces many approaches and interpretive frameworks.

Major Principles in Defining Genre

While it is hard to attempt "a satisfactory universal definition of a genre" (Swales, 2004, p. 29), Sunny Hyon (1996, p. 5) identified some major aspects in the study of genre, including distilling a few key principles. Genre-based work entails negotiating between the "constraint" of the standardized form and the "choice" of the individual author. By concentrating on "discourse competence" and the way that it operationalizes knowledge via genre production, Ian Bruce (2008) recognizes the need to combine linguistic concepts with "pragmatic knowledge and conventionalized forms of communication" (p. 2), a principle that guides our approach of drawing from applied linguistics and rhetorical studies to better understand how genres shape and are shaped by language and the constraints of the underlying argumentative purposes at work in discourse.

Genre is always "colored" by its local context. By applying genre studies techniques to various fields, from legal discourse in professional settings to job application letters in corporate human resources, it becomes possible to note the influence of the respective field on the way texts are constructed (Bhatia, 2014). Regional, cultural, and institutional contexts can shape discourse in radically different fashions. The myriad ways in which academic writers, for example, seek to argue for certain viewpoints and establish academic credibility for themselves remain nonetheless consistent patterns to note, despite contextual differences (Hyland & Diani, 2009).

Genres are "always evolving." Anis Bawarshi (2010) makes several important claims, namely that "genres are *dynamic* because as their conditions of use change" (e.g., technological advancements or disciplinary values), they "must change along with them or risk becoming obsolete" (p. 79). That dynamism, however, should not imply that genres are fleeting or transitory; genres are governed by forces and social expectations of the discourse communities that invent and utilize them to communicate. Janet Giltrow (2002) refers to "durable" meta-genres, or "atmospheres of wordings and activities, demonstrated precedents or sequestered expectations" that accompany a genre, influencing how audiences interact with these texts (p. 195). Meta-genres "patrol . . . and control . . . individuals' participation in the collective, foreseeing or suspecting their involvements elsewhere, differentiating, initiating, restricting, inducing forms of activity, rationalizing and representing the relations of the genre to the community that uses it" (Giltrow, 2002, p. 203).

Just as theorists have posited the existence of larger "meta-genres," providing "shared background and guidance in how to produce and negotiate genres within systems and sets of genres" (Bawarshi, 2010, p. 94), some linguists have focused on the smaller scale, even identifying "part-genre" components, specific sections within the research paper such as methods and discussions (Swales & Feak, 2012). In other words, researchers continue to locate new genres and subgenres with their own respective identifying features. As more genres and subgenres are scrutinized, sophisticated registers and nuanced argumentative styles emerge.

All these identified major aspects inform genre studies, especially for English for academic and specific purposes. Moreover, many scholars in these fields concentrate on addressing the needs of graduate students and English as additional language (EAL) students and practitioners, striving to raise their genre awareness (Burgess & Martín-Martín, 2008). Otherwise, the academy might be denied the fruits of their research simply because, for instance, these novice or multilingual writers do not feel fully conversant in genre conventions of the research article.

The discursive style of academic writing as found on university campuses can remain daunting for newcomers to decipher. Perhaps you have already felt the annoying confusion that comes when a professor assigns a given writing task that you have never attempted before. When incoming students, for instance, encounter a formal academic register for the first time (long before they are required to produce their own drafts), they are often caught up in a bewildering experience of interpreting detailed syllabi, dense textbooks, confusing terms such as "office hours," and obtuse institutional writing, as well as highbrow spoken discourse through professors' lectures. By examining real-life examples of these text types using proven analytical methods, particularly focusing on grammatical variance and lexical features that appear in actual discourse extracts produced by and for academic audiences, students are guided by experienced practitioners to produce these genres (see Biber, 2006).

By reading analysis of LORs written by veteran academics, you can crack the proverbial code of what constitutes an effective recommendation. LORs are not enigmatic documents; they follow established rhetorical and linguistic patterns that, when foregrounded, can become much easier to draft for the anxious academics embarking on their professionalization journey. We wrote this book not just as applied linguists and writing researchers intent on discovering features of under-explored genres, but also as full-time tenured faculty members who write scores of LORs annually; we are also tasked with teaching writing praxis to undergraduate and graduate students. The research informing this book has drawn on our empirical research findings as well as our desire to deconstruct LOR structures and principles for our students and colleagues, including in opinion pieces for professors across various academic disciplines (see Albakry, 2022).

Public vs. Private Genres

As we have established, occluded genres, by definition, are texts that are not available in the public domain. Nonetheless, they are crucial to knowledge production and decision-making in academia. Often specifically written for a small or selective audience, these genres fulfill various important purposes and institutional roles ranging from gaining admission into graduate programs, securing funding support for grants and fellowships, and supporting academic job applications and continued employment. Unlike other academic "open" genres such as research articles or book reviews that enjoy wider exposure (Hyland, 2004a) or some of the genres featured in the *English in Today's Research World* series (Feak & Swales, 2009, 2011), the selected institutional genres analyzed on the following pages are often "behind-the-scenes" texts that are not readily accessible, and, thus, tend not to receive the level of scholarly attention that they deserve. Nonetheless, a close examination of these text types reveals recurrent linguistic features and common rhetorical moves, underscoring their belonging to subgenres that warrant our further investigation.

The term "occluded genre" is more well-established in the existing literature (Autry & Carter, 2015; Hyon, 2008; Loudermilk, 2007; Swales, 1996); and we will occasionally refer to it in this book, along with the term "support genre." We prefer the latter term, however, because it emphasizes the positive, supportive role such genres play in academic careers. An "occluded" genre is also a stronger descriptor for what might be "a declining category" (Swales, 2004, p. 9), given the fact that one might be able to find samples, albeit limited, of any genre on the Internet. Another issue with "occluded," in our view, is that it represents a homogenizing term that could simplify or mask the variance and heterogeneity of this genre group in terms of degree of accessibility and importance.

Both terms, however, reference representative academic texts that serve a basic evaluative function yet are not visible to the public. Because of their level of privacy and writers' lack of familiarity with them, these text types could prove problematic to academics and students who have little to no exposure to them, despite their being tasked to produce polished versions of these genres at critical junctures during their academic careers (Merkel, 2020; Swales, 1996). Remaining unfamiliar with the support genres that may decide their future advancement cannot be beneficial. As Christine Tardy and John Swales (2014) note, genre practitioners often embed "power dynamics" in genres through "gatekeeping practices, intertextuality, or privileged discursive forms . . . [that] exclude users who are unfamiliar with the normalized practices or even those who do not bring the preferred forms of capital to the communicative context" (p. 167).

While outsiders (e.g., proofreaders, reviewers, or copyeditors) may occasionally act as genre "shapers" (Burrough-Boenisch, 2003) within academic discourse, our contention is that the users conversant in these occluded academic text types—those whom Tardy (2016) labels "gate-keepers" (p. 92)—are the ones who actually shape and continually reconstitute the genre, expanding its borders and refining the moves that make every emerging textual artifact a representative example of the genre or subgenre (Samraj, 2014). Therefore, as researchers, we sought to go to the source—documents produced by academic writers themselves—to study the nuanced rhetorical moves and lexical choices in high-stakes academic support subgenres that are still under-explored and thus deserve closer attention. Given their evaluative and administrative importance within the academic system for both professors and students, this exigence provides forceful reasons for more studies to investigate how the thematic, rhetorical structures and textual patterns associated with these genres are constructed and interpreted (Albakry, 2015; Neaderhiser, 2016a, 2016b; Shaw et al., 2014). Plus, landing a teaching position in academia automatically means that you are included in this new club of sorts as a gatekeeper—one whose writing practice shapes how the genre continues to evolve further.

TASK ONE: Is It Occluded?

If an occluded genre comprises those texts not publicly viewable, perhaps due to their confidential nature, go through the following list of actual writing types an academic would be expected to produce over their career, marking "O" for occluded or "N.O." for not occluded.

_____ Assessment/Accreditation reports	_____ Grant applications
_____ Assignment sheets	_____ IRB requests
_____ Bibliographic essays	_____ Job applications
_____ Blogs	_____ Lab reports
_____ Board reports	_____ Letters of recommendation for potential hires
_____ Case studies	_____ Manuscript submission letters

____ CFPs (Calls for Papers for conferences or special journal editions)	____ Master's theses
____ College marketing materials	____ Performance evaluations of employees
____ Comments on student papers	____ Personal statements for teaching positions
____ Conference panel proposals	____ Research articles for peer-reviewed journals
____ Course evaluations	____ Research statements for academic jobs
____ Departmental rubrics	____ Scholarly books/anthologies
____ Doctoral dissertations	____ Statements of teaching philosophy
____ Emails to classes	____ Student grievance reports
____ Essays submitted as assignments	____ Syllabi for courses
____ Faculty profiles on university websites	____ Teaching evaluations of colleagues
____ Faculty senate meeting minutes	____ Tenure and promotion packets
____ Fellowship applications	____ Title IX/Harassment reports
____ Grade reports for athletes	____ University PR campaigns
____ Graduate school applications	

Part of functioning as full members of a college or university faculty involves knowing how to produce the types of texts expected from someone steeped in the discourse community of academia. However, some of these texts are shielded from public view, as well as not taught in the typical graduate program. Mastering these sophisticated writing forms remains integral to an academic's job, as new faculty are often called on to demonstrate expected writing competence of vital academic support genres. Because occluded genres of academic support are rarely taught overtly, the inherent models that writers follow are always held in tension with their own creative innovation as knowledge producers who make specific diction choices in service of the rhetorical arguments that they seek to advance. But making up how one thinks a text in an academic genre should be written will never be as helpful as learning from others with years of experience in writing them.

The field of genre studies continues to expand as researchers uncover more text types that have not been sufficiently analyzed. According to An

Cheng (2018), several academic text types have been subjects of genre analysis to date through an ESP lens, including: theses and dissertations (Paltridge, 2002; Soler-Monreak, 2015), calls for papers (Yang, 2015), grant proposals (Connor & Upton, 2004; Feng & Shi, 2004), conference presentations (Rowley-Jolivet & Carter-Thomas, 2005), and email messages and responses to journal reviewers (Swales & Feak, 2011), to name but a few.

Within the narrower scope of academic support genres, researchers have sought to sketch the breadth of the field (see Neaderhiser, 2016b; Wang & Flowerdew, 2016). Other studies that focused on text types belonging to the category of academic support genres include: manuscript submission letters (Shaw et al., 2014), manuscript reader reviews (Hewings, 2004; Matsuda & Tardy, 2007), graduate application materials (Brown, 2004), dissertation acknowledgments (Hyland, 2003), reappointment-promotion-tenure reports (Hyon, 2008), article and conference abstracts (Lorés, 2004; Yakhontova, 2013), academics' profiles on university websites (Hyland, 2012), MBA "thought essays" (Loudermilk, 2007), and personal statements for graduate applications (Samraj & Monk, 2008).

It is important, however, to specify the differences between public-facing academic genres found in a collegiate setting (e.g., academics' profiles on university websites) and other types of occluded support genres such as manuscript reader reviews and graduate application materials. Moreover, texts can be differentiated on a sliding scale starting with texts that respond to higher-stakes rhetorical situations (e.g., landing a tenure-track teaching position or gaining admission into a competitive graduate program) versus those lower-stakes situations (e.g., grading all student papers via a common departmental rubric).

In light of these categorization distinctions, the LOR genre is a private academic support genre that responds to higher-stakes rhetorical situations. LORs are a commonly accepted component of almost any application process to an academic institution or agency. They form the currency of many academic tenure and promotion packets, awards, grant applications, program admissions, and job searches, as well as research positions that fund dedicated time to complete a major academic or creative work in the applicant's disciplinary field.

The LOR genre has been the object of investigation by numerous journal articles, but it has never received a book-length treatment. Even Swales and Feak's *Navigating Academia: Writing Supporting Genres*

(2011), with its more inclusive and wider coverage, devotes just five pages to LORs (pp. 51–55), clearly indicating the need for further expansion. The present study fills this gap by shedding extensive light on the evaluative discourse of recommendation letters. By focusing on LORs as supporting documents in job and fellowship packages as well as in admission applications, this book seeks to contribute to our understanding of genre knowledge, particularly under-explored academic support genres.

TASK TWO: *Why* Is It Occluded?

If a letter of recommendation (LOR) is occluded, what might be some reasons that you surmise reviewers insist on confidentiality? Under what scenarios could you imagine it would help a selection committee to know that the applicant in question has not reviewed the letter themselves?

_____

_____

_____

Since both parties—the writer/recommender and the reader/ evaluator—often hail from similar fields, the LOR tends to develop common patterns in its formatting and content. LORs, therefore, could be described as a genre of a "typified communicative action" characterized by similar substance and patterns in response to recurrent situations (Yates & Orlikowski, 1992, p. 301). In this sense, they are not much different from other genre conventions that tend to typify, say, business correspondence documents (viz., salutation, opening purpose, details, closing, and signature). What differentiates this specialized genre is its confidential, occluded nature. Not only are these letters confined to the academics who read and write them, but they also are hidden from the view of the applicants on whose behalf they are written, with the exception of digital LORs uploaded to public-facing websites such as LinkedIn and others (Tomlinson & Newman, 2018). Academic applicants are frequently asked to sign confidentiality agreements, which keep them from reading the evaluative content composed by their selected recommenders.

We hope that by reading the following chapters and working through the related writing activities and tasks, you see the veil lift from the major

types of LORs. After becoming familiar with the common content, structures, and language, you should no longer feel intimidated about composing your own academic letters to recommend colleagues or students when
they request them from you.

CHAPTER 2

The Importance and Varied Purposes of LORs

Overview

Every fall or spring, regular as clockwork, academic email inboxes fill up with requests for letters of recommendation. A stellar undergraduate student would like a glowing letter to land a coveted spot in their "reach" graduate program. A graduate student who just defended their dissertation needs a well-crafted LOR that shows them to be equal parts scholar and colleague. Still another colleague has completed a lengthy grant application and now expects your snappy and supportive LOR to seal the deal. No pressure. You are just helping to open career doors or find funding sources that will make a dream project become a reality.

The Importance of LORs

As one of the most important early-stage selection tools used in academia, LORs are an essential component of applications for faculty positions in academic settings. Most academic institutions in North America and elsewhere often require two or more recommendation letters as part of the application materials. These letters are typically written by dissertation advisors, mentors, and colleagues who can attest to an applicant's academic and research abilities, teaching skills, and professional accomplishments. The letters are used, along with an applicant's curriculum vitae, statement of purpose, or cover letter, to evaluate the applicant's candidacy (Aamodt & Bryan, 1993; Lopez et al., 1996) since they provide valuable insights into an applicant's qualifications, achievements, and potential for success.

In vouching for those being recommended, LORs verify information provided by applicants, offer new information about their past performance, and offer an external assessment of their research skills and teaching ability (Madera et al., 2019). For these reasons and given the limited resources and finite funding in academia, LORs weigh heavily when screening candidates for on-campus interviews. Walter Broughton and William Conlogue (2001), for example, found that in terms of importance when screening candidates for on-campus interviews, LORs were ranked among the top four factors including the application cover letter, the potential of making a positive contribution to the institution, and general teaching experience. Other studies (Daniel, 1990; McCarthy & Goffin, 2001) confirmed the predictive validity of the LOR and its status as a significant factor in determining which candidates were hired.

As a means of validating an individual's work, LORs are often used to confirm an applicant's qualifications and accomplishments, particularly in areas where the quality of that person's work might be difficult to assess or because their field of specialization is different from the search members' areas of expertise. They can also provide valuable evidence of an applicant's potential for future success, allowing search committees to identify candidates who are likely to make significant contributions to their field. Given the highly competitive nature of faculty positions, it can be challenging for search committees to assess an applicant's achievements objectively. LORs from academics considered authorities within the field can thus serve as a stamp of approval, indicating that an applicant's accomplishments are legitimate and significant.

In addition to validating an applicant's work, LORs can also highlight their potential for leadership. LORs, for example, can provide insight into an applicant's ability to work collaboratively, lead teams, and mentor others; they do this by providing anecdotes and specific examples to show an applicant's resilience, adaptability, and other interpersonal skills. These qualities are critical for success in academic positions, and LORs can serve as valuable evidence that an applicant possesses these merits.

Finally, letters of recommendation can also serve as a means of advocating for diversity and inclusion in academia, particularly in fields where these issues are a priority. By emphasizing an applicant's contributions to promoting diversity and inclusion, LORs can provide critical evidence of the applicant's commitment to these values, helping search committees identify candidates who are likely to create a more inclusive academic community.

Overall, the importance of recommendation letters lies in their ability to provide a more holistic view of an applicant's qualifications and capabilities beyond their résumé or CV. While an applicant's application materials may provide a summary of their academic and professional achievements, LORs offer a more nuanced understanding of an applicant's skills, work ethic, and character as well as information that is difficult to obtain from other sources. They provide a third-party perspective on an applicant's potential to succeed in an academic role and help search committees make informed decisions about whom to invite for interviews and, ultimately, whom to hire. They are thus crucially important to a junior faculty member's individual success and further career advancements at different stages.

Varied Purposes of LORs

Similar to any writing situation, the LOR invites its writer to consider the audience, the purpose, and the evidence used to make the inherent persuasive claim embedded in the piece. The real-life examples that you will read here cluster around a few typical academic rhetorical situations: being accepted into a graduate program, landing an interview for an academic job, or being considered for a prestigious postdoctoral fellowship. Of course, other rhetorical situations may be imagined (e.g., a fellow faculty member goes up for tenure and promotion), but these three main LOR types cover a wide enough swath of the required LORs to constitute a representative sample, and they will likely be the most common types of LORs you will write for years to come. Reviewing each of the major LOR types, paying close attention to how they accomplish their varied purposes, should prove helpful at this juncture.

A LOR to Refer a Colleague for a Job

Landing a part- or full-time college teaching position can be a daunting process. Whether this first job is viewed as an adjunct position or on the tenure track, you are likely to undergo a challenging interview process. Among other aspects, we will show how personal character as portrayed in LORs written on behalf of academic job applicants, as evidenced in a corpus of actual letters collected from multiple universities, is an essential part in vouching for an applicant.

Given the personal nature of the letter, the writers must show that they have known the candidates well enough to comment on their character and integrity. It would behoove you to think about asking established career academics whom you know personally to write LORs as you embark on your next (or first) job search within academia. We hope that the analysis presented will help you reflect on what type of persona is desirable to project to future institutions to which you plan to apply.

A LOR to Open a Door of Opportunity

As part of developing a robust research agenda, many new academics seek out fellowships at prestigious institutions of higher education. These coveted opportunities to pursue research at world-class establishments are often subsidized by grants that also require lengthy applications. Given the competitive nature of the selection process, committees tasked with making the decision of which recipients receive these rare opportunities often rely on reference letters from experts in the fields.

Like other types of reference letters, LORs for a prestigious fellowship or a competitive grant require recommenders to evaluate the candidate's ability to excel. Moreover, the evaluators usually write as fellow academics in the same field, using the insider perspective to make the case for the candidate's potential success. While not all academics strive to complete a fellowship, these research opportunities provide a means to work on lengthy scholarly projects—often with their expenses paid by grants. With the requirement to "publish or perish," a yearlong fellowship affords qualified applicants the luxury of focusing solely on research that can turn into a publication. As a nascent academic, it is likely that you will request this specific LOR from older mentors whose names are known within their discipline for your own fellowship before you will be asked to write one of these references for others. In any case, it will prove helpful for you to know the specific rhetorical moves and subordinated steps inherent in successful LORs submitted for faculty research fellowships.

A LOR on Behalf of a Former Student

Graduate school presents applicants with a unique set of challenges. Even those highly motivated students who have been coached well and have earned graduate degrees may remain blissfully unaware of the genre conventions that admissions committees will be looking for as they peruse the dozens (if not hundreds) of doctoral-level applications arriving over their departmental transoms. Expecting uninformed students to know what seasoned academics look for in a polished application to a PhD program seems unreasonable, especially when the stakes already feel elevated for neophytes entering a career in academia. Committee members may hold unspoken expectations of what they want to see in a recommendation.

Faculty members are often approached by graduate students to request a letter recommending them for admission to competitive graduate programs. Beyond merely vouching for applicants' proficiency for graduate study, this specific LOR differs slightly in terms of its expectations and conventions. However, few of us are taught explicitly how to navigate the nuances of these high-stakes letters in order to strike a good balance between being truthful and supportive of deserving students without committing misrepresentation. That is unfortunate, of course, because the capacity to write an excellent LOR represents a touchstone for beginning academics that reflects on their writing skills.

The insights in this book will rectify this pedagogical oversight by providing a research-based investigation of this genre. Viewing excerpts of successful LORs that meet different purposes will benefit serious applicants and those recommenders who want to vouch for them without unintentionally casting doubt on their academic aptitude.

TASK THREE: What Do Colleagues Look For?

Below are statements from two college administrators and a faculty member, all of whom are reflecting on the relational qualities of candidates whom they have interviewed. Circle the words where the individual discusses the interpersonal connections that the applicant fostered. On the provided lines, use your own words to describe the characteristics of the ideal candidate they detail.

"In a letter of recommendation, I look for honesty and not just a glowing review. I feel that something is amiss if the recommendation has the candidate walking on water. Sometimes they're too effusive and imply that there's nothing this candidate can't do, and that's just impossible. I read for evidence of real, genuine connection between the recommender and the applicant. I want to see how the applicant worked alongside the seasoned faculty member or assisted with their research in a tangible way to see how well they might function collaboratively on a team in the future." —College administrator

"The ideal academic colleague must excel beyond their scholarship by being pleasant in interactions with others—students, faculty, administrators, and staff alike." —College administrator

"In a recommendation letter for a faculty position, I'd like to see that the writer can balance how much they like the person with a clear-eyed perspective on their abilities and preparation. I also appreciate when there are references to what the recommender knows about the candidate's character." —College faculty member

_____

_____

_____

_____

_____

_____

_____

_____

TASK FOUR: What Do Experts Think?

Below are two statements from veteran faculty members who have served on admissions committees for several years. Underline the words where the individual indicates what they find most valuable in the LOR. On the provided lines, brainstorm some ways that an applicant might demonstrate that trait or aptitude.

"When I read a letter of recommendation for graduate admission, I expect to learn something that is not evident in an applicant's transcripts, test scores, and personal statement. I want to know whether the applicant is teachable: are they motivated to learn and grow as a scholar? I also try to read between the lines to detect any subtle doubt or lack of whole-hearted endorsement." —College administrator

"When reading recommendation letters, I try to read between the lines as there is often implicit social pressure to provide strong recommendations, even if they are not really warranted. I look for evidence that the recommender actually knows the applicant

well. Are they using generic or specific language when referring to the applicant? Do they refer to specific situations or not? Second, I try to get a sense of the real quality of the applicant, beyond the social niceties these letters often invoke. I feel like I am a detective, looking for clues as to what the writer really thinks about the applicant."
—College administrator

Etiquette of Requesting a LOR

Sometimes you will find yourself asking a colleague to write a LOR on your behalf. Likely, you have already made such a request. With hands hovering above the keyboard, watching the cursor blink in the blank email message, or standing just outside their office, wanting both to knock and to walk away quickly without bothering them, you realize that you are adding a burdensome task to their bursting to-do list. Keep in mind, however, that recommendations form the currency of academia. For example, with tenure lines disappearing from many university budgets, the competition for academic jobs grows fiercer annually. Moreover, unlike corporate human resources staff, academic hiring committees (not to mention fellowship selection teams and graduate admissions officers) pore over LORs, carefully rereading lines for any indication that someone might not add the type of value to the institution that they need to find. Your fellow faculty members know this well, so they will rarely begrudge your request for the favor. However, common courtesy dictates that you should give the person both some ample time to complete the task and the right to decline if they cannot make room for it in their schedule. Your failure to plan should not constitute an urgent writing task for any recommender. Similarly, it is always good form to ask permission to use someone's name as a reference. Receiving an unsolicited request for a reference usually does not result in the most glowing recommendation.

Once you have mustered the courage to ask for the LOR, you usually forfeit the right to read its contents—with some exceptions, of course. If the application requires the candidate to build a portfolio of all required documents to send together, for instance, the individual will be able to read the LOR in question. Even if the LOR remains confidential—as most do—the recommender would appreciate receiving any guidelines that were provided for the program admission, the fellowship grant, or the employment opportunity. In other words, it can be helpful to provide the wording of any prompt that the selection committee distributes with the call or advertisement. Occasionally, granting foundations send applicants a hyperlink to a set of helpful tips for recommenders to follow. At the very least, any recommender should receive the individual's CV, information about the opportunity, and a rudimentary outline (written by you) of pertinent details that would aid their writing (e.g., what your upcoming research projects are, the key theorists whose work guides your scholarship and teaching, etc.). Since the writer cannot typically run the draft past you to verify its accuracy, it behooves you to supply anything needful on the front end of the request. Recall the adage "what goes around comes around" in these matters; you will likely be on the receiving end of an LOR request soon enough—even from the very writer you queried to boast of your accomplishments.

Instructor Suggestion

On the day that you assign this reading, consider talking to the class about your own experience with writing recommendations. If you could anonymize and circulate an example of one you recently authored, using such a personalized piece to walk through what you were thinking, how you conceptualized the audience for the piece, and by what criteria you rated the individual, you will lay a foundation for the discussion to come in future class sessions.

CHAPTER 3

Meeting the People Behind the LOR

Sample LOR

The following excerpt, drawn from an actual LOR submitted by a colleague on behalf of a job applicant for an academic position, demonstrates the principles and rhetorical practices outlined in this chapter. Read it over to gain a sense of how this LOR microgenre operates.

> *Dear members of the search committee:*
>
> *I am writing this letter to enthusiastically support [Name]'s application for the position of Assistant Professor of _____ at [Redacted] University. [Name] joined the interdisciplinary program in _____ three years ago after deferring for one year to do a Fulbright Teaching Assistantship in Germany. Since they joined the program, they have without a doubt been one of the most prolific and ambitious students I have met. I have worked with [Name] during most of their time here as their professor, teaching supervisor, as the editor of a journal—[Redacted Title]—for which they have served as managing editor and recently as guest editor, and now as their dissertation advisor. During this time, I have come to know them as a formidable scholar, a kindly colleague, and a devoted member of the community.*
> *. . .*
> *[Name] has a keen sense for how to connect their teaching, research, and community outreach. [Name] is a truly inspiring scholar and teacher. I believe their research will have a lasting impact on the fields*

of _____ and _____ as well as on the many lives they touch through their scholarship, teaching, and community outreach. [Name] works unwaveringly hard in their studies and in everything else they do. I believe they would be a great asset to any program, and I hope you will strongly consider their application.

Please do not hesitate to contact me with any questions about this extraordinary early career researcher and community leader.

Yours truly,

Overview

Most job applicants for academic positions never progress beyond the initial email to a dean, provost, or whomever has been tasked with leading the search committee's work. Akin to the corporate world's online application, the applicant may invest hours in uploading the required materials for a job that sounds promising, only to wait for months to receive a curt reply: "Thank you for your interest in our recent assistant professor position; we have narrowed our field to three finalists, but your application was not deemed a match to our needs at this time."

Frustrating as the anonymity can feel for an applicant, the tension is matched by the hours spent sifting through applications—digital and hard copy—for members of the hiring committee. Over time, favorites rise to the top of the stack. Little by little, the applicants themselves begin to emerge from the pages of various documents (e.g., a cover letter, CV, teaching philosophy statement, or teaching observation form), creating a more three-dimensional picture for the team selecting the candidates to invite for a campus visit, which usually includes a teaching demonstration and multiple in-person interviews.

The LOR substantially aids this process of bringing a real-life person into focus. Reading elegant, snappy letters with memorable anecdotes and colorful descriptions allows committee members to "see" the person in question through the lines that extol their virtues and downplay their vices. The dance inherent in drafting a successful LOR involves revealing just enough about oneself as the recommender to lend validity to the opinion, without overshadowing the applicant being valorized. In this chapter, we examine some of the major "moves" and "steps" involved in this delicate dance known as writing effective LORs.

A Teaching Example

In the following example, taken from the opening paragraph of an academic job LOR, the writer states succinctly the purpose of the letter and highlights their relationship to the applicant for the position, showing how two rhetorical moves can establish logos (the message's meaning) and ethos (credibility to serve as a recommender).

> *I write in support of [Name]'s application for the position of Assistant Professor of Communication Studies at [Redacted] University. I have known [Name] since January 2014 as a doctoral student, then as a co-instructor in a doctoral-level course. We come from different disciplines—[Name] from Communication and me from Adult Education—but I have gotten to know them quite well.*

To the instructor: In your classroom, consider covering the above three-sentence paragraph before introducing (or, more likely, reviewing) move-step analysis. Ask students to mine what information is being conveyed in this section—both the factual details as well as the relational dynamics that are implied. Why would the writer choose to position this content initially in the letter? How does this paragraph set the tone for rest of the LOR?

FOCUS ON RHETORIC: WHAT IS A "MOVE"?

Genre studies owes much of its origin to the exploration of "move analysis" processes (Swales, 1981, 1990), which identify communicative purposes pertinent to a given genre produced by members of a particular discourse community—in this case, recommendation letters. It is a theoretical approach well-suited to genre and analysis—and one tested on different genre types. Locating moves and steps relies on communicative purposes as well as the linguistic features working at the sentence level (Swangboonsatic, 2006).

A move exhibits a particular communicative (or semantic) function (Biber et al. 2007; Upton & Cohen, 2009) made clear when compared to similar extracts in other texts within a given corpus. The auxiliary ways that letter writers operationalize the larger moves in a text, labeled as steps (Swales, 1990), can be considered "rhetorical sub-actions" (Rauen, 2009, p. 58). Once these moves and their subordinate steps are identified, linguistic (viz., grammatical and lexical) elements can be examined using corpus-based discourse analysis techniques, which are less common for genre analysts to draw upon (Upton & Cohen, 2009). It is at this analytical stage that recurrent phrase frames, namely, formulaic and salient phraseological structures (Casal & Kessler, 2020), emerge at key rhetorical junctures in each LOR, indicating that writers rely on particular linguistic bundles to indicate a shift in thought as part of a larger persuasive aim.

Astute learners of the academic LOR genre consider the larger rhetorical moves and subordinated steps operating within each letter and the patterns across the corpus to gauge why particular language choices occur, including the authorial tendency to burnish the credentials of a given applicant through superlatives and other "glowing statements" (Girzadas et al., 1998). Looking at the sentence as the basic unit of annotation allows the careful reader to note how writers use formulaic phrase frames in context to accomplish particular rhetorical objectives (Cotos et al., 2020; Lu et al., 2021). Joseph Afful and Emmanuel Kyei (2020) provide the model for representing every move and step by:

1. Reading each LOR carefully and spotting salient phraseological features.
2. Determining moves and steps from the corpus informed by related studies.
3. Coding the corpus for moves and steps based on the linguistic and discursive functions of the texts.
4. Comparing the inclusion of formulaic phrase frames (p-frames), noting how these phrases operate rhetorically at the sentence and discourse levels.

Table 1: Typical Moves and Steps within LOR Corpus

MOVE	DEFINITION	STEPS / STRATEGIES
1 Opening/ Purpose of Writing	Launching into the promotional genre; explicitly stating the aim of the LOR or softening the approach by an affective move	**Greeting** **Stating purpose**
2 Context of Knowing the Candidate	Function of trust (an ethos-establishing move) based on the length and depth of the relationship between recommender and applicant	**Depth**/capacity of relationship **Length of time known** **Self-positioning** (optional)

Table 1: (Cont.)

MOVE	DEFINITION	STEPS / STRATEGIES
3 Promoting Candidate's Credentials	The writer presents selected information demonstrating qualifications and abilities of the candidate relevant to the desired position, thus portraying the applicant as a worthy candidate.	**Skills** **Previous publications and presentations**
4 Candidate's Personal Values	Character, personality, specific traits, soft skills (can be subsumed in other moves)	
5 Candidate's Contributions to Field	How past publications, presentations, and teaching forecast a promising project—filling a gap and responding to disciplinary trends	**Gap scholarship fills** **Implications of project** **Kairos/exigence** (Move 5 and its steps are optional but common in grant-supporting letters)
6 Providing Needed Background	Salient details about the academic field, including threshold concepts necessary for understanding the applicant's research area(s)	**Disciplinary context** (optional)
7 Polite Ending/ Closure	The writer ends the letter by inviting favorable consideration of the candidate–along with boilerplate features.	**Summative recommendation** Offering further information via standardized statements

PUTTING IT INTO PRACTICE: Letter of Recommendation for Colleague's Job Application

In this chapter, you will follow seven steps to writing a complete job-based LOR.

STEP 1: Invent Your Ideal Colleague.

This exercise will require brainstorming, what the ancient Greek and Roman rhetoricians called "invention." You will need to come up with details to help you write a letter that recommends a fictional person for a job that does not exist. To make things easier, you are certainly welcome to think of a friend in academia (viz., a fellow classmate in graduate school or a colleague with whom you work). Think through these details so that you can compose your eventual drafts with plenty of information.

Name of colleague: _____

Institution where you both worked or attended: _____

In what professional capacity did you meet? _____

How long have you known each other? _____

How well are the two of you acquainted?_____

What is their primary academic discipline? _____

In what competency areas are they experienced? _____

What classes have they taught? _____

What research studies have they published? _____

At what conferences have they presented? What were their topics? _____

What types of campus service have they rendered? _____

How easily do they interact with students? Staff? Other faculty? Administrators?

_____

Choose five character-based adjectives to describe their personality:_____

PUTTING IT INTO PRACTICE: Letter of Recommendation for Colleague's Job Application

STEP 2: Find a Job Advertisement.

To better understand how to reach a specific audience (e.g., a university hiring committee), find a posted job advertisement on an actual university website in the area that your fictional candidate may be applying to (e.g., history, political science, communication studies, visual art, etc.). Knowing how a typical ad is worded will help you tailor your LOR to the perceived audience.

Name of the university:_____

Location:_____

Title of the position:_____

What specific requirements seem mandatory? (e.g., PhD in hand, ABD considered, years of experience) _____

What is the teaching load? 4/4? 3/3? _____

What research/publication expectations are listed? _____

What service expectations are listed? _____

When does the job opening close? _____

Sharing the Context of Knowing the Applicant

A strong LOR demonstrates an underlying relationship between the recommender and the candidate—one close enough to offer a suitable insider perspective of the person's aptitudes and personality traits. Under this ethos-establishing move, recommenders strive to explain the depth and capacity of the relationship shared with their applicants, understanding that many modulated relational layers exist. Enacting this ethos move not only positions the LOR writer as a credible expert on the applicant; it also demonstrates rhetorical fluency that identifies the author as well-versed in the review committee's expectations of this subgenre.

Depth/capacity of relationship

The most common step under the relational move entails the reviewer's highlighting how long and well the writer and the applicant know each other. These relationships could be mapped along an intimacy cline. A few recommenders indicate that they only know the candidate based on their publication record, while others remark about outstanding conference presentations that first caught their attention. These recommenders write about the applicant as a professional acquaintance—an outstanding member of their given field whose work has shaped the discipline—but not as a friend or colleague. For example, one recommender opens the LOR with the following admission: *"[Name] is a major intellect. I don't know [Name] well personally (in fact I met [Name] recently for the first time), but I have long esteemed their writings on historiography."* In a similar strategy, a different recommender uses emotive language to admit their lack of relationship: *"I have not had the pleasure of working with [Name] directly for any length of time, but our scholarly paths have crossed several times, and I have been a close reader of their work (and they of mine)."* By employing the rhetorical device of zeugma (viz., grammatically joining different parts of the sentence), the recommender emphasizes the mutuality of their scholarly relationship and concedes that their relationship with the applicant is limited while simultaneously utilizing the strong emotional term "pleasure." As Jessica Nicklin and Sylvia Roch (2009) have noted, academics often are asked to recommend people whom they do not know well; not only is the unfamiliarity a source of discouragement, but it also may be "detrimental to the usefulness of LORs and to the institution for which the person is being recommended" (p. 88). Clearly, a LOR works more effectively when the reference stems from a deeper relationship—professional and personal.

Closer associations come into view when the recommender and applicant have interacted frequently. Many reference letter writers in our study have written recommendations of their former graduate students. On the other hand, some writers vouch for their former university colleagues, indicating that they worked in the same department. In one particularly long LOR, the writer first informs the review committee that the writer and the applicant enjoy a close relationship. This letter devotes a whole paragraph to describing the nature and depth of their connection: *"I know [Name] quite well. We are both members of a monthly law and philosophy reading group which includes philosophers and law professors from several universities in the [metro] area. [Name] and I also get together fairly often to discuss philosophy one on one in a more casual setting."* This ethos-constructing move attempts to reassure the review committee that this recommender's viewpoint is particularly trustworthy based on their closeness.

Length of time known

The warrant underlying this step is that a longer association means that two parties are closer interpersonally than if they have only known each other for a short time. Recommenders enacted this step by giving a particular year—as far back as thirty years in the past as the earliest date cited in the corpus indicating when the recommender and applicant met. This date also alludes to the applicant's age, positioning the candidate as perhaps more experienced than other competitors. Numerous years were specifically stated within the twenty-first century. For example, one recommender cites a specific year to show the collegiality enjoyed with an applicant from the time the individual worked at the same institution: *"I hired [Name] in 2005 to join our department, and though I have since left [Name of University] for my current position, I have followed their work closely."* All the specific dates mentioned represent some temporal distance from the application's submission date.

TASK FIVE: Length of Relationship

How long should a recommender know the subject of a LOR before writing the document?

_____

_____

What would be the minimal length of time you would need to be acquainted with someone to feel comfortable writing a letter on their behalf? If you are only recent acquaintances or colleagues, how might you counter the objection that your viewpoint is unhelpful?

_____

_____

_____

Some writers resort to quantifying the number of years that they have been acquainted with their respective applicants as a measure of relational closeness. While some recommenders express precise numbers (e.g., *"I first met [Name] exactly ten years ago when [Name] presented a paper on . . ."* or *"I have known [Name] since they completed their doctoral work seven years ago."*), others employ a vague length of time (e.g., "years ago") to reference the acquaintance with the applicant: *"I have known [Name] for almost a decade, first meeting them as a graduate student at my university."* By stating that the recommender knew the person early in their academic career, perhaps the implication is that the applicant has grown significantly over the interim period—growth that the senior scholar is uniquely qualified to assess based on that long association.

The phrase "I have known" or "I've known" does appear in over 30 percent of the LORs studied, framing the nature and duration of the friendship being described. One recommender mentions how the relationship matured from the time the applicant was a graduate student auditing two courses, to the recommender's having the *"pleasure of sitting on their doctoral dissertation committee"* and serving as a "colleague" when the applicant was hired as an instructor for four years at the same college.

The length of time known is not the only way to gauge why someone's opinion should carry more evaluative weight than another's; occasionally prolonged involvement in certain classes or projects means a deeper connection than running into a colleague at a conference or merely following their publications.

PUTTING IT INTO PRACTICE: Letter of Recommendation for Colleague's Job Application

STEP 3: Draft an Outline of the LOR.
Because the most successful LORs for academic positions follow basic rhetorical moves with attendant, subsumed steps, it may prove helpful to map out how you intend to order the elements of the LOR before actually sitting down to write the first draft.

Jot down any relevant information under each move here, realizing that you may have to invent more details from your imagination to have something to say under each move.

Move 1—Opening/Purpose of the LOR: _____

Move 2—Relationship with Candidate: _____

Move 3—The Person's Academic Credentials: _____

Move 4—The Person's Values as a Scholar, Researcher, and Instructor: _____

Move 5—The Person's Contributions to the Field: _____

Move 6—Background on the Individual's Character:_____

Move 7—Closings/Boilerplate Terminology:_____

PUTTING IT INTO PRACTICE: Letter of Recommendation for Colleague's Job Application

STEP 4: Write the Introduction.
  a. Develop a hook for the opening paragraph (move 1).
  b. Avoid using the following phrase: "I am writing to . . ."
  c. Write two or three sentences, without referring much to yourself as the recommender.
  d. Your goal is for your letter to avoid sounding too cliché—as if this person sounds no different than the dozens of other applicants for this position.

Describing Oneself as Recommender

Highlighting a collaboration represents a significant way to imply the trustworthiness of the LOR: any mention of the applicant and writer's having worked jointly on a publication. Collaborating on a research project or even a conference panel requires ongoing communication through emails, conversations, and meetings. A co-authored journal article or edited collection demands careful role negotiation within the relationship. Therefore, when a recommender indicates that *"since our meeting in 2003, [Name] and I have had many occasions to hear each other's work and collaborate together,"* their joint seminars conducted for an annual international symposium provide the arena for mutual respect to grow. In an even more rare rhetorical strategy, the following recommender asserts that in this professional relationship, they are the one with less experience, *"finding their work a great springboard for my own; further, in a special note, I have always found that [Name] is very friendly and has always been encouraging of the work of younger scholars like myself."*

Self-positioning

The recommender occasionally establishes credibility by outlining their own credentials as the letter writer. In nearly a quarter of the letters, writers situate themselves overtly or implicitly as paragons in a given field, thereby validating their role as endorsers, yet the ways that they attempt to conduct this step of self-positioning vary widely from writer to writer. One recommender, given their high-profile editorial position, promises to consider publishing the writing that results from the fellowship: *"As editor of the book series [Z], I will be very interested in considering the applicant's final product for publication."*

LANGUAGE FOCUS: AMPLIFYING CREDIBILITY

Previous studies have researched the use of linguistic credibility amplifiers. When an author backs up claims with specific evidence, statistics, personal examples, or individual anecdotes, these moves operate rhetorically to bolster the trustworthiness of the one writing. Generally, these strategies involve the applicant's "establishing a claim to a scholarly identity" through

---

one's own self-promotion by crediting institutions that were beneficial along the way (Hyland, 2012, p. 72). In the LOR, however, someone else performs this service on the candidate's behalf. By mentioning their own accomplishments (e.g., publications or standing in the field among peers), the LOR writers make the case for why they—respected senior members of a given disciplinary community—should be granted special status as trusted recommenders. These self-positioning statements should not be interpreted as hubris; instead, these instances are implicitly intended to serve as an endorsement of the applicants who are associated with such esteemed colleagues. The danger of talking too much about oneself as a recommender, however, as opposed to devoting most of the letter space to the applicant, is that some readers might infer that the recommender either does not know the individual well enough or has little to say about the strength of their application.

PUTTING IT INTO PRACTICE: Letter of Recommendation for Colleague's Job Application

STEP 5: Draft a Narrative of Collected Information.
   a. Concentrate on the applicant's capacities, scholarly credentials, pedagogical practices, and potential for success in this academic teaching position.
   b. Draft a letter from your outline, starting with information collected in Move 2 from the Step 3 activity.

Providing Disciplinary Background

As a colleague and practitioner in the same field as the applicant, several LOR writers—especially in the fellowship application sub-corpus—supply disciplinary background, theoretical concepts, and key theorists' contributions to contextualize the candidate's research. While they may safely assume that members of the fellowship review committee are fellow academics and administrators, they cannot guarantee that these individuals know as much about a given specific field as the recommenders themselves do. To understand the particular accomplishments that they will cite to corroborate the contention that a given applicant deserves consideration, some letter writers supply disciplinary context (e.g., names of key theorists or writers, foundational notions or ideas, and historization of the field) or stories about the candidates' own findings as budding scholars. Within the corpus, these rhetorical moves nearly always take on a narrative arc—stories that explain key moments within the field or in their development as young scholars or graduate students.

In fields as disparate as European history, sociology, literary studies, and cultural anthropology, the recommenders supply important facts that would require extensive background to contextualize the examples given. From definitions of jargon to simple explanations of abstruse concepts, the recommenders often frame these additions in story form to make them more understandable. For instance, one writer devotes 448 words (two paragraphs) to defending why an early literary critic has been neglected:

> Although [Theorist A] was not an activist in the manner of, say [Theorist B] or [Theorist C], his writing exerted a notable influence on many naturalists and writers, and indirectly on policymakers, activists, and educators concerned with nature, not to mention the average citizen (to judge from the sales figures alone). In this respect he resembles [Theorist D] and, for the same reason, deserves a closer, more informed look.

Notice how the writer relates these facts in terms of a simplified story with a historical angle. In this telling, the audience does not need to know the specifics. Instead, the average reader can grasp the importance of the background, recognizing the need to give an overlooked historical figure another reading. The narrative episodes given to provide context in the corpus are usually narrow in scope, illustrating a particular discovery or a key juncture in the field development of the applicant.

At multiple points, the writers subsume these kinds of narratives, sharing disciplinary context inside another rhetorical move and including content minimally to accomplish the rhetorical aims of another move (ranging from a brief phrase to a succinct paragraph). The writer may seek to identify the applicant as a true exemplar by relating them to forerunners in the field or by explaining the receptivity that they showed as a graduate student under the recommender's supervision. Because background is either given generally (disciplinary context) or specifically (individually regarding the candidate), we maintain that these narratives constitute a rhetorical move, rather than being merely labeled a step under these other larger moves. The story-in-service-of-another-aim approach constitutes a key feature of this type of LOR—one frequent enough in the corpus to suggest that it demonstrates a sophisticated approach to winning over the audience and eliminating any potential objections due to getting lost in dense, formalized language.

Conclusion

This chapter offers an overview of the major moves and steps involved in writing effective LORs. These actions and sub-actions in the letters mark different functions and serve specific communicative functions. The moves and steps, however, are neither fixed nor inflexible. While they do not have to be strictly observed, they can still guide our thinking in composing and organizing recommendation letters.

PUTTING IT INTO PRACTICE: Letter of Recommendation for Colleague's Job Application

STEP 6: Achieve Closure.
  a. Complete the final sentence with an offer to talk further by email, telephone, or video conference should the recipient require additional clarification.
  b. While some boilerplate terminology can be expected, avoid coming across as if you are borrowing the "business-speak" of corporate America. For instance, you need not use the common phrases "at your earliest convenience" or "do not hesitate to contact me."

PUTTING IT INTO PRACTICE: Letter of Recommendation for Colleague's Job Application

STEP 7: Proofread your LOR.
  a. A recommendation follows the accepted conventions of a standard business letter—block-letter formatting.
  b. Brevity is key. Try not to exceed a single page, unless requested to follow a given set of prompts.
  c. Verify your letter's syntax, spelling, mechanics, and grammar by asking someone else to proofread the LOR.

d. One way to catch clunky phrasing in the LOR is by reading the draft aloud to yourself. Anytime that you find yourself pausing at an awkward choice of phrase, circle it for potential revision.

Discussion Questions

1. Why might a selection committee value a recommendation written by someone who can tell stories that include the applicant? Why might this rhetorical move engender more trust?
2. If a recommender devotes too much space in the LOR to describing their own qualifications, how could this approach backfire?
3. Thinking about your own field of study, if you were to recommend someone with your degree, what disciplinary background would you feel inclined to supply? Why?

Instructor Suggestion

The content of this chapter pairs well with the brief section "Letters of Recommendation" in *Navigating Academia: Writing Supporting Genres* (Swales & Feak, 2011, pp. 51–55) from the University of Michigan Press series *English in Today's Research World*. These authors note differences between American LORs (viz., positive, gushing) with their British counterparts (viz., more reserved). Students who hail from countries outside of the United States might appreciate your foregrounding this cultural variation. As well, pointing out these subtle distinctions might lead to a lively classroom discussion on tailoring the message to fit an audience's expectations.

CHAPTER 4

Credentials of the LOR's Subject

Sample LOR

The following excerpt, drawn from an actual LOR submitted by a recommender on behalf of an applicant for a competitive research fellowship position, demonstrates the principles and rhetorical practices outlined in this chapter. Read it over to gain a sense of how this LOR microgenre operates.

> *An intellectually curious person makes a handy friend, as the wealth of their learning and lived experience informs constant, robust conversation and collaboration. It is my extreme honor to write on behalf of someone who fits this description: my dear friend [Name]. I wish to recommend them for the [Redacted] grant. [Name]'s eclectic research interests, breadth of knowledge, meticulous attention to detail, and insatiable curiosity about various subjects (that seems to proliferate into more articles, chapters, and book projects than I would have dreamed one person could draft) make them an ideal candidate for the grant to finish their proposed monograph on _____.*
>
> . . .
>
> *[Name]'s persistence, devotion to a given research task, and insistence that every piece of writing tells a compelling story that reaches its intended audience persuade me that they will excel at feasibly meeting the goal of a completed manuscript within the allotted time. Whatever [Name] sets their mind out to do, they will succeed at it—no doubt in my mind.*
> *As a personal aside, I feel that I must mention what a stellar person [Name] is. While I applaud their many professional accolades (viz., a*

Fulbright scholarship or Outstanding Teacher Award from [Redacted] University), I have come to know [Name] as a generous, humble, and deliberate mentor. Not only did they direct my dissertation research and co-present with me when I was just a graduate student at the [Redacted] Conference at [Redacted] University in 20__, but [Name] has been the most encouraging, supportive voice to me as a nascent academic.

. . .

I urge you to give [Name]'s application for the [Redacted] program the highest possible consideration. I can think of no more deserving recipient.

Overview

Ultimately, the reader of a well-written LOR plans to scan the letter for indications that the person being described has the requisite background, skills, and experience—along with the required degree and training in a certain field—to align well with the opportunity at hand (e.g., a spot in the graduate school cohort, a grant to perform valuable research, or an interview for a faculty role). A LOR differs from a CV, which lists one's accomplishments in chronological order, replete with key dates and even one's grade point average (GPA). The letter, on the other hand, provides a narrative about the person being described, weaving together their credentials to tell a broader story about the kind of individual whose record is displayed on the enclosed résumé. Of course, the trustworthiness of the narrative depends on the length and depth of the relationship between recommender and applicant, an ethos-establishing move.

The writer presents selected information demonstrating qualifications and abilities of the candidate relevant to the desired position to portray the applicant as deserving of the respective opportunity. For example, the recommender will highlight how that person's past publications, presentations, and teaching forecast a promising project to result from this paid research/writing fellowship—filling a gap and responding to disciplinary trends. For a teaching job, the writer may elaborate on salient details about the academic field, including threshold concepts necessary for understanding the applicant's research area(s). In the following chapter, we analyze LORs focusing particularly on the notion of presenting an applicant's credentials.

Presenting Concrete Credentials

Each of the fellowship letters contained in the corpus includes at least one instance of mentioning the applicant's professional credentials, outlining their relevant skills, publications, and presentations, several of which earned awards. Ostensibly, the impetus for the LOR is to distinguish the applicant by commending the respective individual's competence and accomplishments. While tasked with evaluating the candidate's eligibility for a prestigious fellowship, the presumption among recommenders may be that their applicant meets basic requirements. Therefore, LOR writers may be motivated by another communicative purpose: differentiating the applicant from other worthy candidates.

A Teaching Example

In the following example, taken from a fellowship LOR, the writer suggests the scholar's potential contribution and its resulting implications, while supplying necessary disciplinary context, to bolster their chances of being considered for the distinguished award. The first underlined sentence represents the implications of the project, before moving on to highlighting the identified scholarly gap.

> I can attest to [Name]'s scholarly merits by highlighting some aspects of
> their work. Among their contributions, their book on _____ in
> art has been widely acknowledged in their field because of its very
> innovative approach. I do think that this book, together with their other
> publications, offers a great advancement in the field of visual culture.
> [Name]'s theoretical deliberations sustaining the formal examination of
> various products of Asian cultures constitute a very important contribution
> in the field of Asian studies. Noticeably, [Name] is the first scholar to
> establish links between _____ and _____ with Western
> philosophical and phenomenological traditions, thereby bringing about a
> radically new perspective of research.

To the instructor: In your classroom, ask students to note what rhetorical moves are operating in this excerpt, as well as recognizing the level of formality in the language register. How well do they think that this recommender positions their applicant? By what evidence can they make this claim?

Skills

The most frequently occurring step in the entire corpus is unsurprisingly dedicated to outlining an applicant's relevant skills and abilities that indicate the level of scholarship commensurate with the job or fellowship at hand. Many of these skills relate to specific academic fields (e.g., *"[Name] has an old-fashioned ability to create characters"*), while some larger patterns emerge. Read together, these recommenders list the following aptitudes (and more) as fitting multiple candidates: thinking deeply and robustly, researching extensively, handling primary text material carefully, using proven methods expertly, conversing with major theorists and movements, seeking critical feedback on their work, teaching undergraduate and graduate students well, writing articles and monographs that contribute to disciplinary knowledge, and working diligently toward an ultimate goal that benefits the field of study.

While fulfilling the obligatory listing of the candidate's credentials, several recommenders use this step to accentuate the distinctness of the person in question. Corpus analysis helps in providing more insights when words are viewed within their adjacent context. Examining the collocates (i.e., accompanying words) related to the superlative lexical term "best" illustrates this point. Reading the keywords-in-context (KWIC) phrases surrounding "best," including the phrase frame (hereafter "p-frame") "of the best," highlights various rhetorical strategies that recommenders employ to point to why this applicant is singularly deserving of commendation. One recommender's effusive LOR uses "best" three times in the letter, tripling the praise of the candidate (emphasis added):

> *[Name] stands in a very select circle of the* best *graduate students I taught in ancient history during my 45 years in [Name] University.*
> . . .
> *[Name] showed an unusually literate writing style right from the start. And it matured further with every passing year. Their papers were generally the* best *in each seminar they took.*
> . . .
> *[Name]'s performance on the PhD exam was one of the* best *in my memory. They controlled the sources well and showed high skill in marshalling details to establish a general picture. The results were impressive . . .*

In this LOR, the recommender occasionally offers examples that demonstrate how the applicant qualifies for the "best" label, as in the references to qualifying exam scores that compare quantitatively to those from peers. However, at other times, the lexical term "best" is proffered without explanation or substantiation. Notice the demarcation of "45 years" spent teaching at a highly acclaimed university as the way to gauge the recommender's opinion as particularly persuasive.

PUTTING IT INTO PRACTICE: Letter of Recommendation for Academic Fellowship

In this chapter, you will follow six steps to writing a complete fellowship-based LOR.

STEP 1: Do Your Research.

A spot in a fellowship or a postdoctoral program, while rare, provides those fortunate enough to be named a fellow the time to explore a research area more fully or to write a monograph based on previous study. Humanities-related fellowships may vary widely by opportunity, but the selection committees seek assurance that they are making the most appropriate choice based on their agreed-upon criteria.

One such prestigious award is the Fulbright U.S. Scholar Program. These fellowships can involve research or teaching and take various forms based on discipline, specialty, and region of the United States/world. For this scaffolded assignment, visit the website https://fulbrightscholars.org/us-scholar-awards#steps and click on "Letters of Recommendation – required for all applicants."

Read over this information and click on the hyperlinked PDF for even more helpful tips for prospective recommenders.

List five pieces of advice (one sentence each) that Fulbright shares with recommenders to draft their LORs.

Previous/current publications

Most LOR writers in the fellowship application sub-corpus emphasize the extensive publication record of the candidates, interpreting that the fellowship year would be best dedicated to working on a new book, completing a manuscript, conducting research, or turning the doctoral dissertation into publishable form. Achieving publication in a top-tier academic journal or a title at a leading scholarly press carries a significant cache in academe, as shown in examples of this step in the corpus. We do not give specific titles because outlining these works would likely lift the veil of confidentiality. Instead, we examine the arguments constructed around these publications to illustrate rhetorical acumen. How the recommender uses these publications to distinguish their applicant as unusually noteworthy may be obvious from the following excerpt:

> [Name]'s book . . . represents major new thinking on an important topic in Irish Studies. In fact, it is due almost entirely to [Name]'s work that this topic has become central to our understanding of [Name] topic in Irish culture, and European culture generally: [Name] has singled out, defined, historicized, and analyzed a category everyone in Irish Studies knew about but no one had considered with such care and thoroughness. [Name]'s major contribution is in defining the subject, and in defining it in a way that is scholarly, thorough, and original.

This discussion of the applicant's first book does more than just demonstrate that the person can produce publishable content. The inference drawn is that such a first-rate scholar deserves the opportunity to continue to contribute to their chosen field with the kinds of books that can only come by way of the fellowship at hand.

PUTTING IT INTO PRACTICE: Letter of Recommendation for Academic Fellowship

STEP 2: Know Your Audience.

The Fulbright organization offers numerous examples of past projects that their organization has funded. Knowing that fewer than 10 percent of all applicants receive funding, what can you conjecture about the decision-makers who grant these awards? Peruse the philanthropy's website (https://fulbrightscholars.org) to gain a better sense of the stakeholders who would be reading the LORs submitted on behalf of applicants.

Describe the audience and/or some rhetorical choices that you would make when recommending to these interlocutors an acquaintance for a Fulbright fellowship.

Outlining the Applicant's Potential Contributions

Given how beneficial a devoted year could be to advance an applicant's scholarly research and writing, it is unsurprising how many situating moves recommenders make to assure the review committee that the resulting projects/manuscripts are needed, fill known gaps, and promise to be successful contributions. In the corpus, for instance, recommenders often follow the gap step with the implications of the hypothesized project on the field overall. Others employ a sense of exigence, suggesting that the scholarly production cannot afford to be delayed. The implication could be that later discoveries hinge on this publication or that another scholar may "scoop" this work if it is postponed.

Because writers make individualized decisions when composing LORs, some key rhetorical moves that fit the pattern of a successful LOR may be appear along with other moves; in other words, certain writers might combine two or more rhetorical aims within a paragraph to maintain brevity while still trying to persuade their readers on behalf of their subject's merits.

LANGUAGE FOCUS: MINDING THE GAP IN RESEARCH

While the lexical term "gap" may not appear explicitly in the LOR (e.g., "the candidate is familiar with gaps and trends"), LOR writers nonetheless situate the applicant's scholarly work as filling an obvious deficiency in the shared disciplinary knowledge. This sophisticated move has corollaries within academia to the well-positioned peer-reviewed journal article, both "highlighting an absence of research" and "adding to existing research" (Feak & Swales, 2011, p. 81). One writer uses a formal term, "lacuna," to describe how significantly the candidate's scholarship meets a pressing need: *"Much remains to be done on how film shapes the debate, and [Name]'s proposal is aimed squarely at filling this lacuna."* This level of confidence helps the recommender to write persuasively about the applicant's merits. At other times, however, the writer uses hedging language, indicating some hesitancy at predicting that the resulting work will contribute meaningfully to the applicant's field of study. In one letter, for instance, the writer introduces slight doubt regarding the applicant's future work: *"I guess [Name] will take a similar approach in this book"* (emphasis added). This author conjectures that the prospective project, to be potentially funded by a fellowship grant, would likely continue the candidate's previous research, but they distance themselves from making a clear guarantee.

Implications

Given the competitive nature of a fellowship application process, it stands to reason that LOR writers all but promise that the money spent on the potentially deserving recipient will be recouped by the contributions made to the field. In all but two LORs in the corpus, writers imply that the publications arising from the dedicated year of research and writing "will help" or "will be a" boon to the field. More than a dozen tokens of the "will be a" phrase in the corpus are collocated with lexical elements such as "work of the first order," "great success," "volume everyone will use," "outstanding work of scholarship," and "most important book." The writers repeatedly describe an abstract idea yet to be instantiated as a finalized material object (e.g., a book) that carries significant weight within this discourse community. Of course, many of the applicants for prestigious fellowships have already published at least one title, so the likelihood of their producing another scholarly work is fairly high.

TASK SIX: Predicting an Applicant's Contributions

In academia, situating one's scholarly work at the nexus of curiosity and opportunity is commonly called "finding the gap." When someone's study, then, illuminates an area that heretofore has gone unnoticed, the implications to the overall academic community (a network that runs on ideas) are clear.

1. Considering your own discipline, brainstorm a sentence that locates a scholarly gap that a fictional study could fill.

   _____

   _____

2. Imagine that you have published a journal article fulfilling the purpose outlined in the first question. What implications (i.e., consequences, outcomes for future research, etc.) could result from this work appearing in a public setting?

   _____

   _____

   _____

   _____

Two of the most frequently occurring discourse-related keywords to appear in the corpus are semantically linked for academics: "book" and "project." Given that the yearlong fellowship affords scholars time to draft a significant work or to complete the necessary research to write it later without the normal encumbrances of teaching and service, recommenders' emphasizing the resulting book's value is essential for securing the grant. In fact, several LOR writers employ a strong lexical term to bolster the credentials of their respective applicant: the lemma "promise." To be clear, the recommenders do not risk linking their own reputation to another scholar's work by placing themselves in the subject position of the sentences. Instead, the writers refer to the work promising to accomplish important aims for the field, as in these tokens (emphasis added):

- *". . . complete a book that* promises *to make important contributions to current debates . . ."*
- *"This new work* promises *to make a truly unique contribution to the field."*
- *"The project* promises *the kind of engaged ethical study that can be actually useful."*

In several instances, the applicant has already produced a first draft of the book (or at least developed a book proposal) that they plan to revise during the fellowship year. In this case, the LOR writer uses this title, making the implied promise slightly stronger, as this project has taken more definitive shape (emphasis added):

- *"[Title Name]* promises *to be, not the work of a casual reader or dilettante, but rather that of a critically engaged expert in the field."*
- *"[Title Name]* promises *to be an important book, which I look forward to reading and which will certainly interest a wide range of readers."*
- *"[Title Name]* promises *a fine-grained, nuanced analysis."*
- *"[Title Name]* promises *to be written in lively and readable critical prose and to underscore the changes and new directions."*

While this second segment of promise-related lines conveys slightly more convincing language based on precise titles, it should be noted that the transaction of a promise is linked to the publication, not to the person— let alone the recommenders themselves.

PUTTING IT INTO PRACTICE: Letter of Recommendation for Academic Fellowship

STEP 3: Prewrite the Fellowship LOR.

To approximate the real-world writing context, select one of the more than 450 fellowships for which you can write a fictional LOR for an imaginary applicant who has listed you as a reference.

In reading over the particular fellowship in question, and remembering the general instructions given to all recommenders, what key words or concepts should you be sure to mention in your recommendation? At this stage, just get ideas down that you can finesse and sharpen later. This should not be the outlining stage in the writing process. Instead, try to "free write" some ideas that you might develop into mini-narratives or lengthier character descriptions in the final letter.

When to (Graciously) Decline Writing an LOR

Because academic fellowships go to the most brilliant recipients from a talented applicant pool, LOR writers must consider the inherent expectations behind composing them. Institutions that award these competitive grants expect the beneficiaries to bring something valuable to the table—to discover a new insight in research, to deliver a compelling series of lectures, or to mentor younger scholars in their field. Often, these fellowships occur over a very limited time (e.g., one year of dedicated service), so the pressure to produce results is incumbent not just upon the recipient but also upon the recommender.

Not surprisingly, therefore, elite universities and foundations offer suggestions to recommenders for how to frame their letters considering these expectations. For example, Brown University dedicates a webpage to providing tips to recommenders, lest they revert to trite truisms or generic platitudes about their applicant. As an Ivy League institution with a long legacy of stellar research and world-class pedagogy, Brown articulates an understanding of the challenge of being asked to write an LOR for someone who does not show the same promise as others who have met the stringent selection criteria. Stipulating that successful letters require time to be "tailored" to the respective fellowship, these administrators wisely advise saying no to writing a recommendation under the following circumstances:

- You cannot be emphatically positive in support of a student.
- You can't recall much about a student beyond his or her presence in your class and his or her recorded grade.
- You think you are not the best person to write the letter.
- The student approaches you in a highly unprofessional manner.
- You do not have the time or the material to write a good letter.

(Brown University, 2023)

In other words, no recommender should sense an obligation to write a letter, even for the most prestigious fellowship, if drafting such a piece would prove counterproductive. It would be far better for the applicant and for the recommender if the latter was to decline—albeit graciously—such an invitation.

PUTTING IT INTO PRACTICE: Letter of Recommendation for Academic Fellowship

STEP 4: Develop Your Plan.
For this writing task, we will follow the verbatim instructions provided by the Fulbright organization. While the directions may seem simple enough to grasp, the most effective letter writers pore over their prose carefully before submitting their LOR to Fulbright. Even though you are trying to describe an imaginary colleague (and will, therefore, be inventing many of the explanatory details), try to be as thorough as possible in your answers to the following Fulbright prompts (taken from https://fulbrightscholars.org/sites/default/files/2023-03/US_Scholar_LOR_and_FLE_Instructions.pdf). You will work on the first three areas now, reserving their recommended final three points in the next writing task.

- Briefly state how you know the applicant and for how long.
- Discuss the applicant's professional qualifications.
- Depending on the "Type of Activity" listed (there may be more than one type):
  - Teaching: Discuss the applicant's teaching and interactions with students and colleagues in an academic setting. If you are in a position to do so, please discuss their pedagogical approach, course materials, and the effectiveness of their teaching. . . .
  - Research: Discuss potential significance of proposed research. . . .
  - Professional Project: Discuss potential significance of proposed project. . . .

     o Seminar: Discuss how the applicant's participation in the International Education Administrator Seminar will contribute to their home institution's international education goals and their career. If you are the applicant's supervisor, discuss the institutional commitment regarding international education activities and programs.

Advocating for a Rising Star

Occasionally within the corpus, the writers do comment on the trustworthiness of the applicant as a rising star in a given academic field. It should be noted that one recommender lauds their applicant's uniqueness as "promising" in terms of "meeting teaching challenges," linking the individual's accomplishments to a sense of "promise." This use of "promise" as a noun—an inherent characteristic endemic to the applicant—appears in other LORs as well: *"[Name] is a young scholar of exceptional promise, working on what will be a most important book . . ."* Such measured use of exuberant praise could hardly seem remarkable within a genre dedicated to endorsing worthy candidates for an illustrious prize within academia. If one could envision a lexical cline mapping meaning from glowing to modulated to tempered terms (Girzadas et al., 1998), the corpus also reveals a modulated approach to criticism as well. In a single letter, one recommender includes a rare negative assessment: *"[M]y one caveat conceptually, is that I think [Name] should push their thinking further."* Presumably, this suggestion may also underscore why the recommender advises accepting this candidate: The candidate could use the dedicated year to think deeply and research widely the subject area of interest to the field.

PUTTING IT INTO PRACTICE: Letter of Recommendation for Academic Fellowship

STEP 5: Round Out Your Letter.
Once you have written the preliminary information for the Fulbright Scholars LOR, you want to go into greater depth describing the merits of the individual being recommended. The responses to the following three areas (found at https://fulbrights cholars.org/sites/default/files/2023-03/US_Scholar_LOR_and_FLE_Instructions.pdf)

should be lengthier and more detailed than those submitted for the previous writing task.

- o Discuss the potential for impact, including any outcomes and benefits to the applicant's field and home institution.
- o Discuss the applicant's communication skills and their ability to function as a cultural ambassador for the United States, including the applicant's collegiality, cultural adaptability, and sensitivity.
- o Discuss your overall assessment of the candidate. [Here you should feel free to elaborate on their sterling personal qualities outside of their academic credentials and aptitude.]

FOCUS ON RHETORIC: KAIROS

It is noteworthy that a good number of recommendation writers appeal to "kairos," the rhetorical notion of the critical moment that combines timeliness and appropriateness in constructing an appeal for a candidate's work (Bekins et al., 2004). To add exigency, recommenders argue that the respective academic field is ripe for the kind of publication that a particular scholar could produce during the twelve-month fellowship—a work sorely needed in the discipline at this historical moment. A senior professor employs in their letter the adverb "now" twice in a single paragraph to assess a subfield of history as *"only* now *starting to consolidate as a field of scholarly inquiry"* and *"historians are* now *working to connect these social and natural worlds"* (emphasis added). The implication is that the recommended applicant is able to situate their work at this nascent nexus, and thus will be able to seize the opportune scholarly moment well.

In other instances within the corpus, the astute reader can recognize examples of implied kairos, namely, a receptive moment for the ideas generated by the applicant. In one LOR, the writer describes the potential project, adding that *"such a book is eagerly awaited."* Another recommender adopts a more grandiose style in arguing why their candidate should be selected: *"the Institute would allow [Name] to do the field-changing work they were born to do."* This sense that a scholar has come into their own, requiring the fellowship at this pivotal juncture in their career, helps to create the kairotic appeal. In a different example, another LOR writer links the need of the subject area with the need for a dedicated year in a doubled sense of timeliness: *"[T]his is a critical time, and [Name] keenly, and deservedly, needs a concentrated period of time free of exhaustive teaching, advising, and administrative responsibilities."* Given that the typical day of the tenure-track faculty member affords little time for research and drafting, the recommender argues that the fellowship would ensure dedicated intervals to read, write, and revise the work that will advance the applicant's respective field.

To establish exigence, recommenders within this corpus point specifically to time. For example, one LOR writer refers to an emerging "tension" within their given academic area: *"The urgency here has similarly become more complicated, since the scale demanded by the new understandings is much greater—potentially, more of a threat."* Several lexical terms in this statement contribute to the sense of semantic exigence: "urgency," "demanded," and "threat." Each of these domains are sensitive to time. Neglecting an urgent matter of scholarly inquiry does not bode well for society generally, not to mention for the academy. At least one LOR writer attempts to meld multiple kairos appeals into a single proposal to capitalize on the timeliness of their candidate's application:

> *All the pieces are now in place to bring this work to completion, and all that is necessary is the time to do so, which is what the Fellowship will provide. Given the caliber of [Name] and their collaborators, this will be an outstanding work of scholarship; it will find its way into every university library in the world where English-speaking philosophy is pursued and will become the "industry standard."*

Whether this aspiration about the book being available in every university library can be realized is not the point; the intention is to reinforce the importance of the scholar in question.

PUTTING IT INTO PRACTICE: Letter of Recommendation for Academic Fellowship

STEP 6: Smooth Things Out.
At this point, your responses to the Fulbright prompts may sound choppy or disjointed. Reread your earlier responses and work on internal coherence through the use of transitional words and statements. How well can you make the ideas flow together? You may want to move some paragraphs or sentences around to aid in readers' understanding. Keep in mind that the Fulbright instructions themselves may operate as

a suggested outline or template to follow. Deviating too far from this suggested order may cause some selection committee members to find the text jarring.

Write out a full draft of the letter at this stage, along with personal letterhead, the date, inside address of the recipient, an appropriate salutation, block-style body paragraphs, closing, and signature block. Be sure to proofread the text carefully; a single mistake will send an unintended message that you regularly produce shoddy work.

Conclusion

Noting the moves and subsequent steps within letters of recommendation may send the unintended message that an ideal example of this text type must follow a strict rhetorical structure in a particular order. It is important, therefore, to emphasize that the move sequence is not always linear given the fact that some moves tend to be subsumable, as individual recommenders choose to structure the persuasive argument in various ways. One should not assume that the moves must follow a numerical sequence corresponding to Table 1 in chapter 3. Even a fairly simple LOR within the corpus—one where the moves mostly follow in numeric order—cannot be labeled as a template. Noting the patterns of moves and their subsequent steps, along with the use of certain formulaic p-frames to indicate argumentative shifts, however, allows the aberrations to emerge as interesting examples of recommenders improvising on the LOR genre, tailoring the writing to suit the disciplinary conventions or personal stylistic preferences to impress the review committee.

Given the competitive nature of research fellowships and job applications, the occasional use of lexical superlatives to describe outstanding candidates is not surprising. The tendency toward praise, however, may also indicate that all iterations of the LOR genre fit squarely within the epideictic style (characterized by the display of rhetorical and ceremonial skills) (see Tomlinson & Newman, 2018). Whereas the classic model of epideictic rhetoric is the public-facing elegy for a celebrated figure such as a conquering war hero of antiquity, any effort to praise (or even to blame) an individual—especially in service of other persuasive aims such as evaluating their deservedness for a yearlong research fellowship or a tenure-track position—fits this rhetorical genre that focuses squarely on assessing an individual in the present moment.

However, the LOR does not merely act as an effusive encomium or fan letter. These documents also represent a type of evaluative genre, as they attempt to assess the competencies and indications of a candidate's probable future accomplishments (Fortanet, 2008; Hunston & Thompson, 1999). The communicative aim of the LOR genre primarily affirms the applicant's valid candidacy, rendering their significant attributes and accomplishments in a persuasive/promotional manner by citing publications, conference presentations, and teaching positions/skills, while also evaluating the individual's potential for success. The insights provided in chapter 3 and this chapter suggest a fairly stable inherent template that recommenders follow, improvising stylistically and rhetorically on this genre-based model to fit the specific purpose of the recommendation.

Discussion Questions

1. What accounts for the significance of skills being outlined as the most prominent move within the corpus of research fellowship LORs?
2. What composite image could recommenders be trying to portray by detailing the specific skills that a candidate exhibits?
3. Why do you surmise that many LOR writers focus on the implications of the work that would be produced if the applicant were granted the competitive fellowship?
4. What pressures do the committee members shoulder in having to judge the merits of potential competing applications?
5. What factors should a LOR writer consider when supplying the disciplinary context for a more complex project that could mystify the selection committee?
6. When could the attempt to provide necessary background actually undermine the rhetorical purpose of the LOR?

Instructor Suggestions

You may find it helpful when covering the content of this chapter to require the class to do some outside research into LORs for graduate admissions, competitive fellowships, and academic positions. One option might be to request that they use your university's library website to search the holdings for research articles on the criteria used in recommendation letters. Undoubtedly, your students will find more research into medical and dental school admissions and residencies, along with other "hard sciences" opportunities, than their equivalent in the humanities, education, or social sciences areas. Ask students to speculate on why this phenomenon exists. What is inherent to these programs' selection criteria that lends itself to ongoing study and refining? Conversely, why have the humanities, education, or social sciences been neglected by researchers?

On a Lighter Note

Dear Committee Members (2015) is a witty academic epistolary novel written by Julie Schumacher in the form of letters of recommendation. It centers on the main character, Jason Fitger, a disgruntled professor of literature and creative writing in a dwindling English department at the dysfunctional Payne University. He is a prolific writer of recommendation letters, though, and he likes to spend much of his time penning them in order to champion former students or colleagues for different opportunities including employment, fellowships, and awards. Much of the humor of the novel is derived from Fitger's unprofessional behavior in oversharing information and occasionally inserting complaints in his letters of recommendation. Here is an example, which you should never imitate, wherein Professor Fitger is writing to recommend his Payne University colleague, Carole, who is seeking an employment position at a private religious school called Shepardville University:

> Let's consider the facts: Carole is comfortably installed at a research university—dysfunctional, yes; second tier, without question—but we do have a modest reputation here at Payne. Shepardville, on the other hand, is a third-tier private college teetering at the edge of a potato field and is still lightly infused with the tropical flavor of offbeat fundamentalism propagated by its millionaire founder, a white-collar criminal who is currently—correct me if I'm wrong—atoning for multiple financial missteps in the Big House in Texas. You've reinvented yourselves and gone secular, but clearly, in various pockets and odd recesses of the campus,

glassy-eyed recidivists and fanatics are still screaming hosannas, denying the basic tenets of science, and using a whetstone to sharpen their teeth. (p. 124)

It is highly doubtful that Carole will ever get the job at Shepardville University!

CHAPTER 5

The Applicant's Character

Sample LOR

The following excerpt, drawn from an actual LOR submitted by a colleague on behalf of a job applicant for an academic position, demonstrates the principles and rhetorical practices outlined in this chapter. Read it over to gain a sense of how this microgenre operates.

> *Because I have known [Name] in multiple capacities that will be of interest to you in considering candidates for this position, I will speak briefly to all of them.*
>
> *As a professor, [Name] is student-centered, open-minded, and rigorous. That rigor is balanced with kindness and a true investment in seeing their students succeed. [Name]'s specific commitment to working-class students and their knowledge of what these students need to succeed is one of their strongest attributes. I learned a great deal about teaching just from observing them—from seeing them expertly nudge students toward deeper and more nuanced understandings of course content.*
>
> *As a mentor and as my supervisor in the _____ program, [Name] was steady, generous, and insightful. They allowed me to flex my teaching skills in ways that helped me to grow, while always being ready and available to offer guidance and advice if necessary. They are particularly well-suited to lead a discipline that tends to employ multiple levels of pedagogues— from graduate students to adjunct faculty members to full-time lecturers to tenured and tenure-track professors. I especially appreciated [Name]'s guidance as I confronted the challenges of teaching full time, holding an administrative position, and finishing my dissertation. [Name] did not take*

an easy route to academia, and they never seem to forget their roots, even
as we collaborated on writing a manual for new _____ teachers.
I learned a lot from [Name] during the construction of this teaching guide,
and over the years, I don't think I have learned more from anyone else
about the possibilities of _____ instruction and the contextual factors
that might best serve their realization.
I hope that you will take the time to read [Name]'s work and, more
importantly, that you will have the opportunity to meet with them. I'm
sure that you will be impressed by the knowledge, skills, and commitment
they bring to students, to _____, to institutional culture, and to
social issues more broadly.
I would be happy to discuss their qualifications further with you by phone
or email.

Sincerely,

Overview

Whether a politician, a mid-level manager at a large corporation, or an educator, being a person of reputable character remains vitally important. Even in rigorous selection processes such as admission to medical schools, candidates are required to possess the requisite "soft skills" (i.e., relational abilities) that will translate into their eventually being physicians with a compassionate bedside manner. Similarly, in academia, a person may present evidence of a brilliant mind and a promising research agenda, but if they are brusque or standoffish, they will not contribute effectively to the collegial environment that many academic departments strive to achieve. On a more serious note, if the applicant harbors a tendency toward misconduct, then as a university employee, their behavior could prove problematic. Therefore, hiring committees must consider what type of colleague they may be inviting to join the faculty when they begin the interviewing process to fill a vacant teaching spot. In the following chapter, we analyze LORs aimed particularly for academic positions, and to some extent for fellowships and grants, in order to shed light on the different references recommenders make to the applicant's character. It should be noted, however, that character references are also essential in composing other LORs—especially for graduate admission or for a grant or fellowship selection process.

LORs for academic jobs typically focus on the applicants' grasp of disciplinary knowledge, the breadth of courses they have taught, and their scholarly output. References to character are also a long-standing staple in these letters, but defining the domains that "character" covers can seem unclear. Popular business books offer multiple yet confusing definitions of the concept. James Hunter (2004), for example, defines character as "what we are beneath our personality" (p. 142). The definition hints at a universality to character recognizable to anyone who has interacted with its exemplars. It demarcates a difference between "personality" (a subject extensively studied by social psychologists) and "character," a deeper, more durable individualized component that is presumably truer to the individual than mere personality quirks. Yet the concept remains vague and lacks specificity.

TASK SEVEN: What Does Character Resemble?

Think of someone of impeccable character. What words would you choose to describe that person? What virtuous traits do they exhibit?

_____

_____

_____

Based on these examples you know, how then do you personally define "character"?

_____

_____

_____

LANGUAGE FOCUS: HOW TO CATEGORIZE "CHARACTER" TRAITS?

Understanding the linguistic and rhetorical aspects that typify segments of the standard LOR describing a job candidate's character is a fruitful topic that can shed more light on the conventions of the LOR genre, yet it is an understudied area of research (Chamorro-Premuzic & Furnham, 2010). Most of the current strands of LOR research on applicants' character trace back sixty years to a seminal study published by Sherwood H. Peres and J. Robert Garcia (1962) in the journal *Personnel Psychology*. The authors noted 170 frequent adjectives and personality traits in a corpus of 625 LORs and job applications. They specifically examined the attributes of successful applicants for engineering positions, delineating areas that suited this profession.

Based on these attributes, Peres and Garcia's study came up with a taxonomy with five categories: Mental Agility, Cooperation-Consideration, Dependability-Reliability, Urbanity, and Vigor. While providing insightful areas for those working in human resources, the taxonomy was developed mainly for private business and industry jobs. The categories are, therefore, less helpful in reflecting the myriad ways recommenders refer to applicants' character in the typical tenure-track-job search. More than two decades later, Michael Aamodt et al. (1989) validated the results obtained by Peres and Garcia, but they also observed that a "different system" for categorizing LOR traits is in order (p. 153).

A Teaching Example

In the following example taken from an actual academic job LOR, the recommender devotes the final two brief paragraphs to extolling the candidate's personal virtues, as shown in their daily work and in multiple personal interactions:

> As a person, [Name] is positive, lively, ethical, and moral. They have a strong moral compass and an abiding love of others and of community. As a teacher and writer, they are uncompromising in their standards and expectations of self and others. As a role model, they will develop in their students the drive to become better people. Their energy will propel them into a great job as an assistant professor, and, once there, they will be a leader in no time.
>
> In the future, I predict that [Name] will be a leading scholar in our discipline; they will win teaching awards, and they will be an exemplar of service to their college, their discipline, and their community. I recommend [Name] for this position because they fulfill the qualifications, and more importantly, embody the kind of person you want in this job. I hope you will consider them seriously.

To the instructor: In your classroom, ask students to comment on whether any of the language in this excerpt makes them uncomfortable. Why or why not? Poll them on how superlative the tone reads in this letter. Is it over-the-top? Measured? How reticent do they feel to assess another classmate who may be applying for their first academic position?

Values

Despite the letters' inherent objective to vouch personally for the applicant, LOR writers cite personal values or interpersonal characteristics in very few instances, seemingly preferring to praise work-related aptitudes instead. In other words, only occasionally did recommenders comment on the personality traits of the individual in question (e.g., an applicant's "sense of humor"). One outlier, for example, describes the applicant as *"the 'rock' of the department"*—a person known for *"generosity, wisdom, and unrivaled depth of experience."* In the following paragraph, this writer positions the glowing appraisal that ends the letter by *"add[ing] a personal note"* about the scholar's not possessing *"an ounce of pretentiousness . . . [as a] down-to-earth, funny, warm"* person who is a *"delight to work with."* This assessment aligns with a different writer who *"guarantee[s] that many people there would enjoy his company."* These rare descriptions of the character qualities of applicants seem to indicate that the committee could expect a certain level of collegiality that other staid, reserved people may not possess.

In service of their field of study, these recommenders praise applicants' skills. While less explicit than the above example, some recommenders do detail traits that could be categorized as "soft skills": collegiality, liveliness, verve, selflessness, dedication, and curiosity. Occasionally, the recommender feels the need to praise the intellectual brilliance of the candidate: *"[Name]'s one of the best philosophical minds I know."* This statement, written by a senior scholar in philosophy, relies on a mental stratification of all of the experts that the recommender has met, read, or encountered over the course of a long, celebrated career (itself an oblique ethos move). While the recommender may be referring to the applicant's intelligence as evident in conversations, it is clear in the overall letter that the writer refers to written proof of this person's sharp mind: editing a leading journal, writing a book that *"attracted significant attention"* out-side of its delimited area of knowledge, and speaking at the one of the larg-est conferences sponsored in the United States for social scientists. When this writer links an intangible quality such as *"[Name]'s expertise in the history of philosophy"* with a smart mind, clearly the recommender infers that intellectual capacity is a quality every deserving fellowship recipi-ent should embody. On the other hand, various personal attributes in the corpus indicate more about the diligence or grit of the applicant or their stellar publication record: being a person of substance, insight, and origi-nality. To demonstrate the motivation of one candidate, the LOR writer cited *"monkish work habits,"* a hyperbolic, and a bit humorous, phrase suggesting assiduous devotion to research and publication with little supervision needed.

Read as a whole, fellowship/grant letters create the impression that candidates' capacity to produce vital scholarly work matters more than how congenial the person may be. When listing the career accomplish-ments that distinguish a candidate's CV, recommenders are more apt to emphasize work-related skills (e.g., digging deeply into research, using rig-orous methods, publishing widely, consulting on others' writing, or teach-ing undergraduate and graduate courses with aplomb) than relational dynamics. Rather than personality evaluations, which are more notable in job application LORs, the majority of grant LOR writers tend to concen-trate on highlighting the candidates' scholarly research and production.

When recommenders mention positive personal aspects of an appli-cant, they must rely on a set of limited linguistic resources to describe character(istics). Adopting a linguistic approach guided by a framework of character strengths, therefore, could provide a good entry point into examining how character is represented in academic LORs. Informed by Christopher Peterson and Martin Seligman's (2004) Values-in-Action framework of character strengths, our analysis examined the explicit ref-erences to character-related traits to reveal how the candidate's character is portrayed and constructed.

Most specifically, we opted to use broader terms (viz., *intellectual, interpersonal,* and *emotional)* to classify the three germane character strengths, rather than going with the less inclusive and rather outdated labels that Peterson and Seligman (2004) used: Wisdom/ Knowledge, Courage, Humanity, Justice, Temperance, and Transcendence. These imprecise, and sometimes downright mystical, terms share an anachronous ring with some of Peres and Garcia's (1962) labels (e.g., Urbanity, Vigor, etc.). Our modified and more focused version of the Peterson and Seligman (2004) character taxonomy is listed below in Table 2.

Table 2: Renamed Character Strengths (based on Peterson & Seligman, 2004, pp. 29–30)

1. Intellectual strengths	(e.g., creativity, curiosity, love of learning, open-mindedness, perspective)
2. Emotional strengths	(e.g., bravery, integrity, persistence, vitality)
3. Interpersonal strengths	(e.g., collegiality, love, kindness, social intelligence)

This tripartite classification framework provided a lens for locating character-related attributes among the lexical and semantic elements within LORs, evaluating the ways that each LOR writer describes the constitutive personal and interpersonal makeup of the job candidate to vouch for them. Drawing on previous studies (see Aamodt et al., 1989; Chomorro-Premuzic & Furnham, 2010; Ewen, 1998; Knouse, 1983), we closely read the character-related statements of each LOR, identifying lexical terms related to character descriptions and their recurring themes (Hogan, 2005). LOR writers rely on these lexical terms to illustrate their claim that a given applicant demonstrates intellectual acuity and curiosity, emotional maturity, and interpersonal and social skills.

TASK EIGHT: A "Triple Threat"?

In the world of the theater, a talented actor may be described as a "triple threat" because they can act, sing, and dance, ensuring that they would add value to any musical production that would cast them. In an academic setting, the triple threat that seems to matter to LOR writers is the person who possesses strengths in three domains: intellectual, emotional, and interpersonal. Looking over the qualities outlined in Table 3, what could be the possible outcomes if a hypothetical hiring committee were to hire a new assistant professor who was strong in just *one* of these domains while being grossly deficient in the other two?

Sole Character Strength Area	Potential Positive Outcomes for the Hiring Department	Potential Negative Results for the Hiring Department
Intellectual		
Emotional		
Interpersonal		

The analysis reveals that while only a small fraction of the letters in the corpus confines themselves exclusively to the professional accomplishments of the candidate with little personal information added, the vast majority of the letters contains references to the applicants' character. Interestingly, the character descriptions seem to be clustered in the final paragraph(s), often prefaced as a "personal" aside about the individual characteristics of the applicant. Not only do these character descriptions sound distinct from the rest of the LOR, but they also cover vastly different content than the recitation of austere arenas of publications and teaching loads. Therefore, prefacing these comments with a phrase including the lexical term "personal" allows the LOR writer to signal that they are shifting the subject matter from academic performance to the respective individual's attributes. These asides often demonstrate a marked shift to a more personal and involved style from the previous delineation of the applicant's publications, teaching responsibilities, and accomplishments in the earlier paragraphs.

Close reading and coding of these character sections enabled us to identify which character-trait adjectives appear more frequently within the LOR. Using the frequency list generated by the concordance software, we further coded the data to assign them into the three categories of character strengths (see Table 3).

Table 3: All Character-Related Adjectives in LOR Corpus

Intellectual Adjectives		
1. (Above) Average	16. Extraordinary	31. Penetrating
2. Accomplished	17. First-rate	32. Practical
3. Advanced	18. Formidable	33. Prepared

(Continued)

Table 3: (Cont.)

Intellectual Adjectives

4. Analytic	19. Gifted	34. Principled
5. Analytical	20. Hardest	35. Serious
6. Articulate	21. Highly-organized	36. Sharp
7. Catholic (not religious)	22. Ideal	37. Skilled
8. Clear	23. Informed	38. Smart
9. Consistent	24. Insightful	39. Sterling
10. Consummate	25. Intelligent	40. Superb
11. Creative	26. Knowledgeable	41. Talented
12. Critical	27. Nimble	42. Top-notch
13. Curious	28. One-of-a-kind	43. True
14. Dedicated	29. Organized	44. Well-organized
15. Emerging	30. Pedagogical	45. Well-spoken

Emotional Adjectives

1. Accessible	13. Ethical	25. Passionate
2. Ambitious	14. Full	26. Personal
3. Committed	15. Greatest	27. Poised
4. Confident	16. Happy	28. Positive
5. Conscientious	17. Hard	29. Same (*work ethic*)
6. Determined	18. Hardworking	30. Selfless
7. Difficult (*handles difficult challenges*)	19. Honest	31. Self-driven
8. Disciplined	20. Humble	32. Tireless
9. Down-to-earth	21. Imaginative	33. Ultra-efficient
10. Efficient	22. Mature	34. Unflappable
11. Energetic	23. Modest	
12. Enthusiastic	24. Motivated	

Interpersonal Adjectives

1. Astute	17. Fellow	33. Outstanding
2. Best (*brings out the best in others*)	18. Finer	34. Personable
3. Better	19. Friendly	35. Pleasant
4. Challenging (*overcoming challenging situations*)	20. Funny	36. Possible

Table 3: (Cont.)

Interpersonal Adjectives		
5. Collaborative	21. Generous	37. Professional
6. Collegial	22. Genuine	38. Reliable
7. Considerate	23. Helpful	39. Respected
8. Courteous	24. Impressive	40. Similar
9. Deep	25. Inspiring	41. Strategic
10. Devoted	26. Intensive	42. Student-centered
11. Eager	27. Intercultural	43. Supportive
12. Easy *(to work with)*	28. Lifelong *(impression)*	44. Thoughtful
13. Egalitarian	29. Lucky	45. Valuable
14. Excellent *(people skills)*	30. Nice	46. Valued
15. Face-to-face	31. Noted	47. Well-respected
16. Fair	32. Organizational	

To ensure that we were isolating descriptive lexical items, we went through the frequency list of keywords in context (**KWIC**) to isolate all the adjectives—whether single-term adjectives or hyphenated adjectival phrases—used by LOR writers. We then narrowed them down to the terms that referred to the candidates themselves, rather than the prospective job opportunity or the campus where they trained as graduate students. We were then able to assign each lexical term to one of the three character-related categories based on their semantic reference.

It needs to be noted, however, that some terms would occasionally fit two overlapping character categories (e.g., labeling an individual "honest and open" can straddle both emotional and interpersonal domains). The general adjective "great" could contextually encompass all three character-related categories. In the example *"[Name] is someone with a great head and a great heart,"* for instance, it is applied to the applicant's "head" (i.e., intellectual strengths) and "heart" (i.e., emotional strengths), as revealed through the individual's interpersonal relationships. Because such descriptive words can operate linguistically in a broad fashion, we eliminated them from the process of categorization into one of the discrete categories.

Figure 1 below conceptualizes the most frequently mentioned character-related domains. By linking the most common adjectives that recommenders use to describe established components of character, the figure maps out how academic writers conceive of positive character attributes. It can be viewed as a composite representation of the stellar character traits of academic job applicants that would be most germane to a general open faculty position in academe.

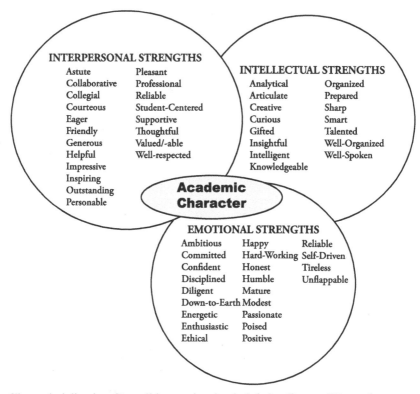

Figure 1: Adjectives Describing an Academic Job Applicant of Exemplary Character

---

TASK NINE: How the Notion of "Character" Changes over Time

In the decades since Peres and Garcia's 1962 publication of a list of actual terms that recommenders used to describe outstanding job candidates, certain words or phrases have acquired unpleasant associations. Others come across as too personal for a workplace evaluation. Review the following actual terms, considering why they seem dated today. Remember, these human resources administrators were living in a different era marked linguistically by terms that contemporary readers would deem old-fashioned or downright problematic today. On the line next to each item, list possible negative connotations or describe what "red flags" may be raised by encountering such a term in a recommendation today.

Big-hearted _____

Chatty _____

Clean-cut _____

Hustling _____

Well-bred _____

TASK TEN: "Are We Hiring a Superhero?"

Looking over the traits within the three circles of Figure 1, it is obvious that no one will excel in all of these areas simultaneously, unless, of course, they also wear a cape and can leap tall buildings in a single bound. If one job candidate cannot embody all aspects of academic character perfectly, why might it be nonetheless helpful for the members of a hiring committee to see the range of attributes that recommenders use to describe ideal applicants?

_____

_____

PUTTING IT INTO PRACTICE: Other Academic-Related Letter of Recommendation
In this chapter, you will try your hand at writing three specialized types of LORs.

Building on the knowledge that you have gained through reading the sample texts within this book and from drafting your own versions of the various LOR subgenres, write the first text type of three in this chapter, following rhetorical conventions and developing a letter that recommends an imaginary candidate for the following honor typically reserved for candidates with outstanding academic potential.

TYPE 1: Scholarships
Certain agencies or philanthropies offer scholarships—especially for study-abroad programs while in undergraduate or graduate school. These may cover tuition, room/ board, textbooks, or other expenses.

Intellectual Strengths

Analysis of LORs' mention of character traits reveals a great deal of overlap among our core character strengths (viz., intellectual, emotional, and interpersonal domains). One should not be surprised that an academic faculty position requires an intelligent individual—one who has earned a terminal degree in their field of study and can handle the intellectually rigorous demands of teaching and research. However, measures of intellect and intelligence, as conceptualized by LOR writers in the corpus, seem to exceed a simple IQ assessment. LOR writers within this corpus create a semantic field of intellectual strengths congruent with Peterson and Seligman (2004), but investigating the context—what other character traits were collocated with intelligence/brilliance—as well as asides, lists of attributes, and anecdotes provides a nuanced view of what recommenders mean when they reference a colleague's intellect. It cannot be sufficient to select the brightest, most accomplished individual for an open position. If a candidate is both smart and hospitable to others, they may have an advantage in the selection process.

By accentuating the applicant's personable character, LOR writers temper the notion that intellectuals tend to be inhospitable or arrogant. For example, one writer includes a reference to the candidate's interpersonal affability:

* *"On a personal level, [Name] is very friendly and easy to get along with. . . . They have the intelligence, work ethic and desire needed for [this position]. Furthermore, given their attitude, they will constantly raise the bar both as a teacher and as a colleague."*

By introducing this aside with the phrase "[o]n a personal level," the LOR writer accomplishes two tasks: bracketing the relational competence from the applicant's professional qualifications while implying that the two arenas overlap, indicating the writer's own eligibility to comment on the candidate's character. In other words, this recommender has signaled their credibility to remark about the applicant's intelligence because they have also observed such traits (e.g., friendliness, ease in interacting with colleagues, hard work ethic, etc.) that only come through in a longer-term association at a personal level. In effect, this aside functions as an ethos-related appeal to the hiring committee, coming at the end of the LOR to leave a lasting positive impression of the candidate's character.

Recommenders also carry out character-related impression-building within the corpus by listing traits or qualities that they consider equivalent in value to intelligence, a characteristic that seems particularly prized by an academic hiring committee. The following extract resembles the earlier one, as it indicates that the writer has saved the personal domain for the end of the LOR to extol the intellectual virtues of the person whom they are recommending for the position:

- *"I would be remiss, in summing up, if I did not also speak to [Name]'s sterling personal qualities. They are manifestly intelligent and talented, with an infectious enthusiasm, filled with exciting ideas and insights. But they are equally, and genuinely, modest and abidingly humble. They are possessed of the* sine qua non *of the true intellectual: the desire to persuade and the willingness to be persuaded."* [emphasis in original]

Not only has the recommender reserved comment on the applicant's character for the conclusion of the LOR, but they have also incorporated the adjective "sterling" to modify the examples that follow—chiefly intellectual strengths. The phrase "manifestly intelligent" implies that the applicant's acumen is readily apparent upon first meeting them. The adverbial "manifestly" suggests that tangible material products (e.g., books, research articles, or conference presentations) stand as monuments to the applicant's intellect. The addition of the word "talented" conveys both the applicant's creativity and curiosity, as well as the drive to polish these inherent abilities in outstanding ways. Still, Peterson and Seligman (2004) distinguish inherent talents and competencies from actual character strengths (p. 80). It is in the second half of this trait-filled description that the recommender differentiates the applicant from a presumed perception of intellectuals as aloof by adding that *"they are equally, and genuinely, modest and abidingly humble."* Placing humility on the same plane as intelligence, the recommender comments obliquely on a perceived common deficiency of academics: the humility to admit what they do not know. Adding the intensifiers "genuinely" and "abidingly" carries earnestness as well in emphasizing how "modest" and "humble" the person in question comes across in real-life situations, albeit without a clear example. Finally, the invocation of a Latin phrase in place of a single-word equivalent (e.g., "essence" or "epitome") makes its own subtle logos appeal: This writer is also intelligent and classically educated, making their opinion worth attending to carefully. The final trait of this applicant's character, *"the desire to persuade and the willingness to be persuaded,"* underscores the importance that rhetoric plays in any academic endeavor.

Even when merely listing intellectual strengths along with other character-related traits, the LOR writers in this corpus broaden notions of what intelligence means outside of simply cognitive capacities. Several writers use the simplest grammatical structure of /Subject + "to be" verb + (adverbial-modified) adjective/s to list attributes that include the candidate's intellectual strengths, as shown in the following examples:

- *"They are reliable, knowledgeable, well-spoken, and thoughtful in their consideration of the work of their colleagues."*
- *"They are smart, adaptable, and a first-rate problem-solver."*
- *"They are creative, forward-thinking, engaged and, most of all, a wonderful teacher. If I had a full-time position available in [academic field], I would offer it to them in a heartbeat. Their insight and skills are superb, and I believe that [Name] will make an ideal teacher in any program lucky enough to have them. You will find them to be open, curious, incredibly hard working with a nimble and penetrating mind."*
- *"They are thorough, consistent, insightful, and analytical."*

Even in merely listing intelligence-related attributes, recommenders hit many of Peterson and Seligman's (2004) listed traits, including curiosity, creativity, open-mindedness, and innovation. Moreover, these LOR writers expand intelligence to suggest other characteristic features, including collaboration (*"thoughtful in their consideration of the work of their colleagues"* and *"extremely good at listening, works to build consensus"*); problem-solving with complex puzzles (*"smart, adaptable, and a first-rate problem-solver"*); progressive thinking (*"forward-thinking"*); and analysis (*"a nimble and penetrating mind"* and *"analytical"*). These carefully chosen lexical items suggest that the LOR writer understands the demands of working within a faculty that places professors on committees to work toward common goals or to solve conundrums that arise. As well, the college campus often considers complex issues well before society at large encounters them, rendering the "forward-thinking" colleague an asset. Being able to analyze effectively (viz., break down complicated matters into understandable components) makes one a helpful academic professional as well.

These trait lists also appear in the corpus in slightly more nuanced syntactic constructions that nonetheless function similarly to the statements made with the "to be" infinitive verb forms. For example, one recommender implies that inviting the job candidate to campus will result in a pleasant discovery related to their intellectual strengths: *"You will find them to be articulate, distinctively above average in intellect, poised, talented, and personable."* A hiring committee might expect an applicant with an earned doctorate to be highly intelligent, but this writer makes a distinction by implying that the candidate in question is smarter than their peers vying for this position. However, that brilliance is tempered by a personal "poise" (perhaps exhibiting a measure of self-control in social situations) and "personability," suggesting that this above-average applicant does not lack social graces, despite being the smartest person in the room. Being able to distinguish an outstanding job candidate from the pool of capable applicants comes across as being helpful—as if the recommender has offered to make the hiring committee's task easier.

Praising the applicant's intellectual ability is often paired with their communicative skills in the context of the relational domains of teaching and mentoring. One recommender offers the following example as an illustration: *"It should be clear from my assessment that Dr. [Name] is intelligent and has sharp critical and analytic skills. Moreover, they have excellent communication skills, honed through their teaching and their mentoring."* Any character-related capacity that can be "honed" through practice allows the hiring committee to deduce that the applicant remains committed to personal improvement. Such an individual also qualifies as an exemplar to fellow faculty and students, as evidenced by their willingness to mentor others. Mentoring occurs in pedagogical relationships naturally; some universities also tap faculty to act as official mentors to new hires. In the latter sense, the experienced person shows the new arrival the ropes of teaching at the institution. In either form, an ideal mentor's character may be described as more than merely intelligent, as in the following extract: *"Their consistently thoughtful demeanor no doubt extends to their teaching, as it would to mentoring as well.*" The notion of "thoughtfulness" is rich etymologically: Not only does it convey a wise person who thinks deeply on topics, but it also suggests compassion—the empathy to stay attuned to the felt needs of others, a quality commensurate with a healthy mentoring relationship.

Another way that LOR writers link intellectual strengths with interpersonal intuition is through including an anecdote that highlights the applicant's actions in a given situation. The following excerpt that gave us the inspiration for this chapter significantly illustrates the use of anecdotal evidence:

- *"No letter of reference is complete without a few words about the candidate's personality. The usual good properties easily apply to [Name]: they are a smart and nice person, a good team-member, generous with their time and ideas when it comes to students. But one property that I would like to emphasize is their strength of character. As I mentioned, they overcame considerable difficulties to reach the point of [disciplinary] sophistication where they are, as they came in with considerably less background than their classmates. They worked hard and in an environment that can be quite demanding. . . . [Name] is determined and they are strong. I think they have many good things ahead of them."*

Again, the recommender reserves the final paragraph of the LOR for an explicit character reference, emphasizing how deserving the applicant is to be considered for the open position. This writer includes an interesting phrase that reads, *"The usual good properties easily apply,"* suggesting the possibility of an internalized template that recommendation letter writers follow when composing the LOR. The specific aforementioned capacities, however, are not throwaway terms; these attributes (smart, nice, collaborative, and *"generous with their time and ideas when it comes to students"*) paint the picture of a sociable person who uses their intellectual strengths for the benefit of the campus community. It is the emphasized attribute "strength of character" that helps to bring a nuanced perspective to the notion of intellectual strengths. The LOR writer references an earlier story outlined in a previous paragraph about how the candidate came to graduate school without much of the prerequisite training of their classmates, putting them at a distinct disadvantage. Nevertheless, they overcame the educational obstacles and attained the types of scholarly success as a doctoral student that would indicate a promising career with *"many good things ahead of them."* By placing the candidate in a circle of scholars of intellectual "sophistication," the recommender shows they value hard work as a true indicator of intellectual strength.

TASK ELEVEN: How Recommenders Describe Intelligence

Teaching at the collegiate level certainly requires a person with a sharp mind. However, when writing the LOR for a professor job, no recommender would consider it prudent to list the applicant's IQ (intelligence quotient). Instead, they rely on nuances of language and well-chosen anecdotes to indicate that someone is smart.

Look over the excerpts above, then make a list of five phrases used to describe someone's intellectual strengths:

_____

_____

PUTTING IT INTO PRACTICE: Other Academic-Related Letter of Recommendation

Building on the knowledge that you have gained through reading the sample texts within this book and from drafting your own versions of the various LOR subgenres, write one of the following rhetorical conventions below, developing a letter that recommends an imaginary candidate for the following honor typically reserved for outstanding academics.

TYPE 2: Awards/Recognition
Many colleges offer awards to a top student or faculty member recognized by a committee. These awards often are accompanied by financial remuneration, especially if an endowment helps to underwrite the award.

Interpersonal Strengths

Academia regularly produces exemplary scholars, but not every one of these nascent graduates stands out in terms of interpersonal strengths. Instead, their excellence shows up in publications or conference presentations. While these accomplishments fill out one's CV, being known as a stand-out colleague makes the distinction all the more noteworthy.

The following LOR writer employs superlative constructions to highlight the outstanding qualities of their applicants—in this case relationally:

- *"I can think of no one in the field of [academic field] that I would rather work with, and I have benefitted immensely from those collaborations in which we have already engaged."*

By broadening the scope of potential picks to the pool of all scholars within a given field in the humanities, this recommender has lauded their job candidate as unusually amiable and cooperative. Even though this description does not qualify the phrase *"I have benefitted immensely from those collaborations,"* it seems safe to assume that the recommender refers to advantages beyond shared bylines on academic articles. Perhaps the writer also counts a close, collaborative friendship based on mutual respect as one of the benefits. Moreover, the writer leaves open the possibility of further joint research ventures in the future with the phrase *"in which we have already engaged."* This writer would likely welcome future combined projects.

Most of the other recommenders represented in this corpus describe ways in which the people whom they recommend add to the overall ambiance of their departments using terms such as "collaborative," "colleague," and "community" to reference a job candidate's interpersonal strengths—together effecting a sense of robust collegiality. Because faculty members rarely co-teach courses or hold rank over one another beyond the honorific titles assigned to their tenured status (e.g., assistant, associate, or full professor), their opportunities to engage in interpersonal relationships within the hierarchy of academia come from committee assignments or taking an interest in their fellow department members. Therefore, the day-to-day work of the typical faculty member is hard to conceptualize as "civic" involvement. However, a colleague who chooses to collaborate with others by sharing pedagogical or classroom-management ideas, rather than acting in their own self-interest, helps to contribute to the type of collegial community that mutually benefits all of the faculty involved. When someone exhibits a genuinely warm, hospitable affect toward others with whom they work, they are often deemed as a trusted "colleague" who acts in a "collegial" manner, even contributing to a harmonious workplace "community." The term "collegiality" seems to depict this interconnectedness well.

The ideal academic colleague, as one of the letters explicitly states, must excel beyond their scholarship by being pleasant in interactions with others—students, faculty, administrators, and staff alike. Peterson and Seligman (2004) expand the domain of "interpersonal strengths" to include an inherent "humanity . . . that involve[s] tending and befriending others" by exhibiting the following traits:

- Love: *Valuing close relations with others, in particular those in which sharing and caring are reciprocated; being close to people*
- Kindness: *Doing favors and good deeds for others; helping them, taking care of them*
- Social intelligence: *Being aware of the motives and feelings of other people and oneself; knowing what to do to fit into different social situations; knowing what makes other people tick (p. 29)*

The descriptions of applicants' character within the LOR corpus bears out this distinction: Recommenders place high value on the ways in which these job candidates tend to interact in kind, considerate, and helpful ways as proof for their interpersonal competence. Being easy to get along with carries a certain cache in academia, as evidenced by the following excerpt:

- *"They are highly intelligent, extremely good at listening, work to build consensus, and are very good company. . . . [They have] excellent people skills."*

Not only does this individual seem amiable and compassionate—even demonstrating active listening skills—but they are also known for pleasant interactions. Since faculty offices are often spaced close together, enabling ongoing conversations in the hallways between colleagues, a person who is enjoyable to be around for lengths of time carries a certain value as a fellow professor. This individual seems to exhibit two of Peterson and Seligman's humanity subareas: love and social intelligence. Knowing the social expectations and meeting them in other-centered ways sounds akin to another applicant's description in the LOR corpus:

- *"On a personal level, [Name] is a genuine pleasure to be around. They are well liked and well respected by the faculty and their fellow students. They are quiet at times but also can assert themselves when necessary."*

Qualifying as *"a genuine pleasure to be around"* implies taking a sincere interest in others' welfare. Someone exhibiting a narcissistic personality or an intellectually arrogant air would not fit this description.

This recommender gestures toward another of Peterson and Seligman's character strengths: *temperance*, specifically humility/modesty: "not seeking the spotlight" (2004, p. 30). This description, however, foregrounds the applicant's "social intelligence," the phrase that Peterson and Seligman (2004) prefer over "emotional intelligence" or "personal intelligence" for "its interpersonal relevance and . . . moral flavor" (p. 299). Socially intelligent people would rarely act manipulatively toward their coworkers. They can both read the room, remaining quiet while others banter about their ideas, as well as *"assert themselves when necessary."* This interplay between listening to others' input and contributing meaningfully shows a collegial sense of interdependence with one's potential coworkers.

Several of the recommenders adopt a deferential tone when describing applicants' interpersonal strengths, as if to elevate these individuals above their peers in these relational domains. In the following excerpt, one imagines various interlocutors to whom the writer compares the job candidates—people who practice lesser altruism:

- *"Interpersonally, [Name] is egalitarian in their interactions, creative and funny when those qualities are warranted, and they are not driven by ego. They are principled and disciplined and willing to seek the best ways of doing things even when the best is not the easiest [route]."*

Higher education institutions are fraught with hierarchical relationships, as well as tenure-based positions. An "egalitarian" person would stand out amid others who could be jockeying for a position. This person also gauges situations to know the best time to inject brainstormed solutions or welcome humor and when to refrain. By identifying them as a "principled and disciplined" person who will avoid the "easiest" route, the recommender heightens the perception of the applicant as purposeful and mature, leading from a sense of personal integrity. Being simultaneously principled and personable must be rare, as shown by another recommender who sets up an interesting contrast in describing their applicant:

- *"[Name] is hard working, serious of purpose, and ambitious, but they are also selfless and kind, and they are always considerate of the thoughts and feelings of others."*

Completing a terminal degree that makes one eligible for a tenure-track faculty position requires a serious drive. Ambition, however, can lead one to seem egocentric or self-centered in motivation. The candidate referenced above, however, apparently does not allow their career aspirations to dilute their compassion. By listing the character quality of kindness, this recommender taps the connotations of "generosity, nurturance, care, compassion, and altruistic love" as exhibiting behaviors that others might deem "nice" (Peterson & Seligman, 2004, p. 326). To bolster this connection, the LOR writer glosses the terms "selfless and kind" as their being "always considerate of the thoughts and feelings of others." By not clarifying the referent for "others," the implication is that the individual respects students, staff, faculty, and administrators—all levels of institutional hierarchy. This tendency to avoid responding relationally to perceived hegemonic power dynamics on campus also conveys interpersonal strength.

TASK TWELVE: How Recommenders Describe Relational Skills

Joining the faculty at any university means working in close proximity to other colleagues when planning curricula, serving on committees, directing research projects, etc. Therefore, recommenders tend to emphasize how easy someone is to work with and that they get along well with others.

Look over the excerpts above, then make a list of five phrases used to describe someone's interpersonal strengths:

_____

_____

_____

_____

PUTTING IT INTO PRACTICE: Other Academic-Related Letter of Recommendation

Building on the knowledge that you have gained through reading the sample texts within this book and from drafting your own versions of the various LOR subgenres, write one of the following rhetorical conventions below, developing a letter that recommends an imaginary candidate for the following honor typically reserved for outstanding academics.

TYPE 3: Tenure and Promotion (T&P) Packets

The T&P LOR microgenre deserves slightly more elaboration. After academics have served at a particular institution for a set period of time (i.e., customarily six or seven years), they are invited to apply for tenure, a status that is meant to protect their free speech rights on campus and to ensure them a continuing teaching contract. Along with tenure usually comes promotion to the next academic rank (e.g., from assistant to associate professor), perhaps along with a salary increase. A major factor in determining whether a faculty member is tenurable is performance in the classroom. Be sure that your fictional LOR features narratives related to the individual's pedagogy.

Emotional Strengths

In the following excerpts, the LOR writer explicitly states that they are switching to "a [more] personal level" of the reference letter:

- *"In addition to all of the above qualities, and on a more personal level, I find [Name] to be a pleasant person with an enjoyable sense of humor."*
- *"On a personal level, they are friendly, well organized, energetic, and most definitely hard-working."*

In the first instance, the reference to the applicant's "pleasant" personality and humor are an addendum—tacked on at the end of the letter after exhausting the more concrete qualities (e.g., classes taught, areas studied, and articles published). It could be inferred, perhaps, that pleasantness stems from the well-adjusted personality of a person in touch with their emotions. The writer of the second excerpt, on the other hand, does detail the candidate's "personal" aspects. Of course, these character strength categories overlap and combine. For instance, friendliness might belong to "interpersonal strength," while being "well-organized" may be a sure sign of a person with a sharp mind. The reason why this excerpt is germane to emotional strengths is the doubling of qualities that typify a work ethic: *"**energetic,** and most definitely **hard-working**"* (emphasis added). An energetic person possesses the vitality, namely, "zest, enthusiasm, vigor, [and] energy" that helps them produce the rigorous workload maintained by the usual academic, as well as "infectiously energize" those around them (Peterson & Seligman, 2004, p. 273). This candidate would likely be described as "wholehearted" and "passionate." It is the invocation of the so-called "Protestant work ethic," so central to the American sense of being rewarded for putting effort into important pursuits, that links this applicant to courage. Moreover, labeling the "hard-working" quality with adverbs such as "most definitely," the LOR writer intensifies the recommendation to demonstrate how sincerely they feel this depiction to be true. In this way, the writer resembles the following recommender who piles on the praise of an applicant of exemplary intellectual, interpersonal, and emotional strengths:

- *"Moreover, [Name] is a highly organized person. They plan everything well and always complete work on time. As someone who is intelligent, friendly, ultra-efficient, hard-working, and full of energy, they work well both individually and within a team."*

The key to this litany of positive attributes is their being *"ultra-efficient, hard-working, and full of energy."* Industrious job candidates will likely distinguish themselves as accomplished colleagues down the road. Their inner drive serves them well in an academic career.

Speaking of accomplishments, some academics exhibit a reserved perspective about celebrating their achievements. As a result, their brilliance may escape notice. One such example comes in an extended description of an applicant who might otherwise fly under the radar:

- *"The second personal note concerns their demeanor. [Name] is incredibly modest and quiet about their accomplishments. But you should not be deceived: [Name] is one of the hardest working researchers in [academic discipline] that I know. And they know how to target their research efforts to focus on issues and considerations that matter (rather than simply logging a lot of hours). And finally, they apply this same work ethic to their teaching. They might not come across as impressive in an initial meeting. But if you dig a little deeper, I am confident that you will be highly impressed by their abilities."*

In as many words, the LOR writer shares a truism: "Don't judge a book by its cover." The refusal to boast about one's achievements should not be interpreted as a negative aspect. By using a superlative construction (viz., *"one of the hardest working researchers . . . I know"*), the writer emphasizes the perseverance of the candidate and their willingness to persist despite any impediments. The obstacle remains unspecified, but it may be shyness or the unremarkable first impression that they make. By adding the conditional statement (viz., *"if you dig a little deeper"*), the writer all but guarantees that such exploration (counter to any false first impressions) will pay off. Beyond an outgoing personality, this potential colleague will courageously put in the work that it takes to succeed.

Such a successful potential colleague might be differentiated from the pool of applicants by an LOR that uses the exact wording from Peterson and Seligman's character strengths classification. The researchers identify "integrity" as one of the subareas of courage, differentiating from authenticity and honesty by its adherence to "moral probity and self-unity," evoking the connotations of wholeness from the term's Latin roots (Peterson & Seligman, 2004, p. 250). Therefore, when a recommender uses integrity within their character reference, its presence becomes meaningful, as in the following excerpt:

- *"In addition to their practical experience and knowledge, Dr. [Name] will bring to their work as professor personal qualities including integrity, fair-mindedness, and a sense of humor."*

The LOR writer may not intend to rank the qualities that they seek to laud in the applicant, but the placement of the term "integrity" first may suggest the importance that the candidate places on this virtue. Being a moral exemplar also constitutes courage, as in this snippet from a different LOR: *"They are flexible and agreeable, and they demonstrate strong ethical standards."* This recommender has packed quite a bit into this compound sentence. A person with unyielding ethics, who refuses to kowtow to compromising standards, might otherwise be presumed to be rigid in their belief system. However, the LOR writer celebrates the individual's flexibility and agreeable nature, pointing out that the applicant holds these character traits in tension admirably.

TASK THIRTEEN: How Recommenders Describe Emotions

Working within the stressful environment of higher education places demands on faculty. Even in a workplace setting where employees would choose words very carefully when describing a colleague (lest they be considered inappropriate), what terms do LOR writers typically resort to using when describing a grounded, well-adjusted applicant?

Look over the excerpts above, then make a list of five phrases used to describe someone's emotional strengths:

_____

_____

_____

_____

Another recommender crafts a similar rhetorical move: listing several outstanding character qualities that one might assume would be contradictory but are not. This LOR writer, however, waits to the end of the correspondence to make this pronouncement:

* *"In sum, I know that [Name], PhD, to be an informed, committed, self-driven, enthusiastic, tireless, and valued colleague whose [academic discipline] research and work benefit the discipline and community."*

This word "tireless" appears twice within the corpus. Its connotations include an indefatigable drive. It also implies an impressive scholarly output, produced with few complaints. In order to bring maximum benefit to the institution and to themselves, this applicant ties "accomplish[ing] goals in the face of opposition, external or internal" with the betterment of others (Peterson & Seligman, 2004, p. 199). The archetype of the driven person may be someone who will push themselves at all costs to achieve the pinnacle of their career goals, but truly exemplary candidates regard the needs of the larger community before their own. This type of altruism fuels self-denial in the most exemplary of job applicants.

TASK FOURTEEN: Writing an Academic Job LOR

NOTE: The following letter is not intended to serve as a template for writing your future letters. Rather, this example allows us to annotate different sections to analyze how each part operates rhetorically to persuade the hiring committee to consider the applicant's merits. As you read over this generalized LOR, see if you can assess what each paragraph adds to the overall recommendation before checking the footnotes.

Dear Administrator:

When selecting a faculty member to teach [disciplinary field)] courses in, it quickly becomes apparent that the ideal candidate is experienced, highly regarded, and adaptable to new situations. I wish to commend [Name], my former colleague from [Redacted] University, as just such a stellar educator whose background, training, experience, and knowledge will add tremendous value to any institution fortunate to offer them a teaching contract.

[Name] has taught an impressive array of courses during the many years that they have been employed at [Redacted] University. Their CV ranges from first-year to graduate courses. As a trained scholar with an earned PhD from [Redacted] University, [Name]'s strength lies in breaking down complex topics[LOR 1] of [various examples] for students to grasp. Because they also maintain a passionate commitment for teaching international students, they have often taught courses with many ESL and L2 speakers enrolled.

In these various [discipline]-based courses, [Name] brings cutting-edge theory as well as proven teaching methods born from years as a full-time tenured faculty member [or bright, adaptable adjunct instructor/lecturer]. Their dissertation concerned a thorough examination of [specific area of research]. Their research results were so convincing that their dissertation became a monograph in their field.[LOR 2] They have shown me the importance of concentrating on students' basic needs.

Similarly, [Name] invests in the lives of their students. [Cite examples of service.] In this capacity, they have acted as a mentor,[LOR 3] helping launch some of the brightest graduates of our university into their own graduate programs and positions in academia and the private sector.

Personally,[LOR 4] I can guarantee no instructor will work harder than [Name]. I have seen them juggling a 4/4 course load, grading dozens of papers, developing online courses, conducting department assessments, and serving as a diligent assistant professor, all while applying successfully for tenure. They thrive when working with people of various demographic and ideological backgrounds. Their ethical standards are impeccable. I have always known their demeanor to be thoughtful, deliberate, and unflappable. Their laid-back personality means that they will function well in the department that chooses to hire them; you will appreciate how little oversight they will require to thrive in this position.[LOR 5] Any institution where [Name] serves as instructor of record will benefit from an educator of their caliber.

Sincerely,
[Recommender's name and institutional affiliation]

Now that you have read this fictional letter and checked the annotations (i.e., footnotes indicated in the running text), what does the recommender hope to leave as a final impression of the candidate in question—particularly after reading the final paragraph?

_____

_____

_____

[LOR 1] Here the LOR writer emphasizes the job candidate's intellectual strengths—as the capacity to teach complex concepts requires a mental agility and communicative dexterity that are highly prized in the academy.

[LOR 2] How the writer illustrates the intellectual capacity to apply research findings speaks to the candidate's overlapping domains of intellectual and interpersonal skills. It is one thing to conduct an exemplary, robust research study. Successfully implementing results gleaned from such a scholarly investigation into one's pedagogy shows a relational savvy needed in today's higher education classrooms.

[LOR 3] By referring to the applicant's experience as a mentor to struggling/developing students, the recommender covers the important area of interpersonal strengths—beyond commenting on their perceived sense of collegiality among the department faculty.

[LOR 4] The lexical term "personally" signals a rhetorical shift in the LOR. What follows reads as an assessment of the applicant's emotional strengths—including aspects of their inherent character, amiable personality, and work ethic. By placing this paragraph at the conclusion of the letter, the recommender uses this final move to convey a favorable impression of the person in question as the final memory invoked.

[LOR 5] This line matters significantly. While all new faculty require some orientation and training to the specific ways that a respective campus operates, knowing that a person can be self-motivated, organized, and curious enough to work with "little oversight" provides a huge boon to the overburdened faculty mentor, department head, or academic dean assigned to assist their transition.

TASK FIFTEEN: Describe Someone Else's Character

Using at least two related adjectives from each area above (e.g., intellectual, emotional, and interpersonal), **write a final LOR paragraph** (of no more than three sentences) highlighting the character of a friend, colleague, or classmate as if they were applying for an academic teaching position.

_____

_____

_____

_____

_____

TASK SIXTEEN: Describe Your Own Character

Using at least two related adjectives from each area above (intellectual, emotional, and interpersonal), **write a final LOR paragraph** (of no more than three sentences) that you hope a recommender would say about your character if you were applying for your ideal academic job.

_____

_____

_____

_____

Beware of Gender Bias

Given that LORs are commonly used as selection tools in academic employment, many studies looked at gender differences and the extent of gender bias in how men and women are portrayed in reference letters (Akos & Kretchmar, 2016; Madera et al., 2009). Unlike our empirical study with redacted names, these studies investigated LORs without removing information about the gender of applicants and thus were able to systematically code and interpret gender differences. It is important to note, however, that most of this work has been conducted in the science, technology, engineering, and math (STEM) disciplines—particularly in the biomedical fields focusing on applications for surgery fellowship and residency programs (Dutt et al., 2016; Filippou et al., 2019; French et al., 2019; Sarraf et al., 2021; Trix & Psenka, 2003). Most studies that explored the gender gap (see also Hoffman et al., 2020; Turrentine et al., 2019) have identified patterns of consistent bias in LORs written for men when compared to women. The gist of these studies is that a potential bias against female applicants could manifest itself in differential language use particularly involving adjectives and other subtle language resources that may sow the seeds of doubt.

Drawing on the social role of theory of sex, the results of Juan Madera et al. (2009) indicated that women applying for academic positions were described in LORs by using character-related adjectives that were more group-oriented and related to their ability to build rapport with others. Men, by contrast, were more likely to be described using adjectives portraying them as more task-oriented, assertive agents with a higher individual capacity to act independently. This could lead to different perceptions of applicants. As the authors argue, responsibilities in the academic setting have historically been defined by norms that are more tied to traits of individual agency, such as being independent, self-confident, competitive, authoritative, etc.—traits that are more stereotypically associated with men than women (see Bailyn, 2003).

Another difference related to variations in adjective use as documented in the literature include the finding by Frances Trix and Carolyn Psenka (2003) that LORs for men are more likely to note accomplishments (e.g., "successful," "knowledgeable") and less likely to employ what they call "grindstone adjectives," that is, adjectives that put more emphasis on effort and inherent ability rather than achievements (e.g., "hardworking," "conscientious," "diligent," etc.).

Finally, Carol Isaac et al. (2011) found that LORs written for female (versus male) applicants for medical school residency placement contained more doubt raisers (i.e., phrases or statements that question an applicant's aptness for a job) and what they call "tentative" words and phrases (e.g., "she might," "it is possible she could"). The same conclusion was reiterated in another Madera et al. study (2019) published in the

Journal of Business and Psychology (for more details on doubt raisers, see chapter 6).

These patterns of linguistic usage related to gender differences could negatively affect how applicants are evaluated, since they signal that the person being recommended is either less independent or that the recommender does not have an entirely positive impression of the applicant and is less than certain about her. In other words, these differences potentially perpetuate bias in LORs and can put women applying for academic positions at a relative disadvantage compared to their male counterparts. However, these findings do not necessarily mean that there is any nefarious intent to harm female applicants on the part of letter writers. In fact, some studies (e.g., Colarelli et al., 2002) have found that male recommenders wrote more favorable letters for female versus male applicants. As Kuheli Dutt et al. (2016) point out, the apparent bias seems to be shared since LORs for women appear to vary systematically in tone relative to their male counterparts regardless of whether the reference letter is written by a male or female recommender. The variation in language use, then, could point to the presence of implicit biases that may operate beneath the level of conscious awareness.

When writing a letter of recommendation, it is important, therefore, to be more reflective to avoid any gender-biased or sexist language. By ensuring that the letter does not contribute to discrimination or unequal treatment, we can avoid unintentionally undermining a qualified candidate and hurting the chances of those who seek our support. To avoid the cognitive pitfalls and linguistic traps of gender bias, here are two simple guidelines that we should bear in mind when writing such LORs:

1) Focus on accomplishments and skills: Center your letter on the candidate's achievements, skills, and abilities rather than their gender or appearance. We should avoid making biased assumptions based on gender or gender stereotypes, and we should strive to focus on the candidate's qualifications and achievements (e.g., teaching awards, roles in leadership, publication record, presentations, scholarships, grant funding, etc.) (see Hargrove, 2022).

2) Avoid gendered adjectives: We should be mindful of using any potentially gendered language that could reinforce gender stereotypes: for example, adjectives such as "aggressive" or "assertive" for men and "nurturing," "caring," and "compassionate" for women. In general,

we should strive for inclusive language that reflects the diversity of the community.

LORs can serve as a means of advocating for diversity and inclusion in academia. Given the systemic inequalities that exist within academic institutions, it is essential to ensure that we are evaluating applicants fairly and equitably. Guarding against unconscious biases and promoting equality and inclusivity can help ensure that our reference letters are fair and unbiased.

Conclusion

In reviewing the corpus-based findings of this chapter on character statements, one result bears underscoring: Moralistic value judgments about the character of individual applicants were largely absent and replaced by a broad-minded sense of what constitutes character. None of the statements within the corpus comes across as particularly intrusive or overly moralizing. Rather, the writers land on a more humanistic, secular way of defining (or at least realizing) character. For instance, a job candidate who is lauded as *"demonstrat[ing] strong ethical standards"* is—in the same sentence—praised for being *"flexible and agreeable."* Similarly, a candidate who is praised for being "honest" is also described as "open" and willing to disagree amicably. Character, at least as these LOR writers have envisioned it, maps onto semantic ideas more related to collegial neighborliness rather than religious or moral matters of perceiving right and wrong. In other words, recommenders emphasized universal nonsectarian notions of character that would likely be shared across the pluralistic milieu of the contemporary university campus.

A letter of recommendation must accomplish a hefty purpose: vouch for the academic credentials of a qualified applicant, while also describing the individual's character strengths in such a way that would make that person seem winsome, personable, and collegial. Teaching positions demand long hours in often cramped office spaces, usually in proximity with colleagues subjected to the same stressful, demanding conditions. An accomplished academic who folds under pressure or whose ego becomes paramount in their career does not help create a good work environment. Given the competitive nature of academic job searches, it makes sense that the bulk of the LOR content lauds the typical applicant's grasp of disciplinary knowledge, the breadth of courses taught, and the number of scholarly publications amassed. The character-related paragraphs, often located in the final section of the written recommendation, describing the applicants as amiable, bright, hardworking, and enthusiastic, however, should not be deemed a peripheral afterthought. These character descriptions, often prefaced as "personal" asides, might, in fact, be the most important information the LOR writer shares to influence the hiring committee.

Discussion Questions

1. How would you define the word "character" in the most capacious way possible, respecting various faith traditions and cultural backgrounds?
2. Comment on how you can refer to an applicant's "intellectual strengths" in an LOR without resorting to discussions of the applicant's IQ. In other words, what attributes help round out a three-dimensional depiction of an applicant's intellectual credentials?
3. How do emotional strengths help to determine resilience?
4. What part of the academic career relies on faculty members' embodying interpersonal strengths? What can happen if a brilliant mind lands someone a faculty position, but they are stunted interpersonally?

Instructor Suggestions

Of all the chapters covered in this book, the content on writing character references stands to potentially make students squirm. Moreover, talking about their hesitancy in the larger group could add unintentionally to their discomfort. To mitigate this risk, perhaps assign a short reflective paper asking students to explore how qualified they feel to describe others' personalities, their strengths and weaknesses, and the corresponding fitness for academic service. Another idea that highlights the fallibility of character references would be to outline cases when the flowery language used to describe supposed exemplary colleagues could backfire under suspicion of their alleged misconduct. Students might appreciate a nuanced discussion of the following article: "The Frenzied Folly of Professorial Groupthink: A Dust-Up Over an Open Letter Signed by Star Scholars Reflects a Troubling Trend" (2022) from *The Chronicle of Higher Education* (URL in References).

CHAPTER 6

Softening and Strengthening Modifiers

Sample LOR

The following excerpt, drawn from an actual LOR submitted by a colleague on behalf of a job applicant for an academic position, demonstrates the principles and rhetorical practices outlined in this chapter. Read it over to gain a sense of how this microgenre operates.

> *I'm writing to highly recommend [Name] for the tenure-track position as Assistant Professor of _____ in _____ at [Redacted] University. [Name] has been teaching here at [Redacted] College for two and a half years and is now teaching for their sixth semester. I cannot say enough about what a wonderful contribution they have made to our undergraduate students, especially the way they came and "took over" courses to replace our recently departed colleague.*
>
> *. . .*
>
> *[Name], through their own infectious enthusiasm, has also managed to galvanize a small but dedicated group of _____ majors into meeting weekly—for no credit initially—to share research interests, and to get constructive feedback both from [Name] and from each other. I have sat in with this group a couple of times and was delighted both with the wonderfully friendly atmosphere and also the level of seriousness and display of analytic skills.*
>
> *. . .*
>
> *I have visited several of [Name]'s classes and was impressed in several ways: by their concern to make sure students had understood concepts*

taught in the previous class—they collect anonymous feedback at the end of each class, which can include questions and comments about the subject matter, as well as suggestions relating to their teaching style. In addition, [Name] writes a brief outline of the day's topic(s) on the board at the start of class and encourages the class to be fully involved, especially by asking students at random for their comments or questions.

In their first senior seminar, [Name] was introduced to a small but fairly diverse group of students, including both _____ majors and also some doubling in Education. Some students were able to keep up with the readings and understand the concepts, whereas others had significant struggles, one even being reduced to tears in class. When this happened, [Name] demonstrated what to me is a wonderful sense of compassion, went over to the student, put their hand on their shoulder, and assured the student that together they would work through the material and successfully navigate the course.

Overview

It is important to investigate the language of LORs in different academic programs, particularly in how these important documents pave the way for younger scholars to be admitted to graduate school. These advanced degrees serve as important thresholds to academic or research careers, so the required LORs function as tickets to open doors.

This chapter focuses on the subsection of our collected LORs that were written as part of applications for admission to different PhD programs in large, comprehensive universities, and here we identify some of this LOR type's salient linguistic and discursive features. The approach that we explore in this chapter addresses the question of evaluative linguistic resources (e.g., modals and adjectives) and mitigation strategies, noting how they encode appraisal information and indicate a recommender's level of confidence, or lack thereof, in an applicant's ability.

Doubt Raisers and Certainty Markers

The letters were initially examined using WordSmith concordance software tools to investigate the lexical profile through word lists and their frequency order. We then noted the frequency of common lexical items that could signal as markers of appraisal expressing positive/negative attitude (Martin & White, 2005, p. 2) as well as the frequency of the eight central modals ("will," "would," "may," "might," "can," "could," "should," and "must") and their contextual usage within the corpus (see Biber et al., 1999, p. 483). The appraisal framework of J. R. Martin and Peter R. R. White (2005) serves only as an overall interpretive guidance; we do not necessarily follow its terminology or its full taxonomy that covers the attributes and wide range of nominal and verbal appraisal features.

LANGUAGE FOCUS: READING BETWEEN THE LINES OF THE LOR

For the items in the lexical profile, the focus, besides the modals, was more on the most common content words—exclusively adjectives. Interestingly, very few explicitly negative content adjectives, if any, appeared in the lexical profile. For instance, words such as "poor," "inadequate," or "unsatisfactory" were totally absent from the corpus. Since the corpus search method proved insufficient in capturing the presentation of salient words with negative or potentially negative orientation, we also relied on close reading and qualitative/pragmatic analysis that entailed underlining and coding of positive (i.e., adjectives signaling praise) as well as negative orientation. Negative orientation is operationalized here as any statement or presentation that could potentially raise doubt about the applicant's ability, level of intelligence, academic preparedness, and/or work ethic, informed by the general category of doubt raisers (Trix & Psenka, 2003, p. 203).

As identified by Trix and Psenka (2003), there are four sets of doubt raisers: negativity, faint praise, hedges, and irrelevant information. As an example of negativity, a recommender might describe an applicant as someone who "does not have much teaching experience" or is "not the best student I have had." An illustration of faint praise would be describing an applicant as someone who "needs only minimum supervision" or "is better than average." A hedging example would be a statement like "the applicant appears to be highly motivated," while an irrelevancy would be describing the applicant as someone who "enjoys hiking" or is "active in church." If we rank these categories on a scale from more negative to less negative, outright negativity will rank first followed by hedging—which is still a forthright doubt raiser. In the third place will be faint praise—which can be interpreted as a backhanded compliment—followed finally by irrelevancy.

In our analysis, however, given that our focus is more on identifying the common syntactic formulas that encode the expression of any negative/potentially negative presentation, we combine all these semantic markers in a broad category of (potentially) negative information.

A Teaching Example

In the following example taken from an LOR written for admission to a prestigious graduate program, the writer boosts the aptitude of the applicant while admitting that they still have room to grow as a scholar.

> [Name] evidenced extraordinary scholarly skills during their years at [Redacted] University. Their writing shows the capacity to make a compelling claim backed by appropriate, researched evidence and an astute analytical ability, albeit sometimes still requiring some copyediting attention. [Name] has a sharp mind and a winsome personality. They adapt very well to new circumstances, as shown by their work teaching elementary school in South Korea. They purposely applied to this teaching role to gain valuable international experience, in preparation for their future career aspirations in international law, particularly to address the inequities in the expenses that diabetic patients have encountered—a disease that they know all too well. They would like to serve in public office or as a lobbyist representing patient-centric, healthcare policy organizations. I can see them readily achieve this career goal, provided they receive the high-caliber education that only your graduate program can offer them.

To the instructor: In your classroom, ask students to rate how highly this recommender considers this potential graduate student. As evidenced in the letter: Where does the candidate display strength? What potential weaknesses do they possess? Upon what specific phrases do students base their opinions?

Markers of Adequacy and Markers of Excellence

For a more fine-tuned analysis of praise-signaling adjectives, positive adjectives were divided into two categories: markers of excellence and markers of adequacy. Markers of excellence are the words that imply superiority in an applicant's ability and set the applicant apart from others. Such words are distinguishable from others in that they also imply a standard, which has been surpassed, or a difference from other possible applicants (e.g., "superior," "superb," "extraordinary," etc.). These markers can be defined in a more general category as being words which imply "better than good" (good+) or "better than the standard" (standard+). The word "extraordinary" could perhaps provide a good illustration: There is a norm or baseline ("ordinary") and the indication of being above the norm level ("extra"). The markers of adequacy, on the other hand, could be represented as "equal to standard or good" (standard= or good=), for example, "good," "fine," and "solid." These adjectives are examined in the contexts in which they occur.

TASK SEVENTEEN: Markers of Excellence vs. Adequacy

Language is fascinating, in that often a writer can indicate an opinion without coming out explicitly in fawning praise or harsh criticism. Instead, through verbs called "modals," recommenders can gesture toward a stellar candidate or one who may not be the best fit for the position, despite their being requested to write the LOR that committee members are reading.

In the hypothetical statements below, underline the modal verbs (forms of the lemmas "will," "can," or "shall") before circling whether the statement describes the individual as excellent ("E") or adequate ("A").

When pressed for a description, I would have to mention their tendency to be a lone ranger.	E or	A?
I could see them succeed as a professor if someone were to mentor them extensively in the role.	E or	A?
They should be a stronger researcher at this stage of their academic career.	E or	A?
If I could select a single person who forecasts where this field is heading, I would definitely choose [Name].	E or	A?

How do you know if a writer may be indicating a candidate of superlative merit or merely a satisfactory choice?

_____

_____

_____

_____

PUTTING IT INTO PRACTICE: Letter of Recommendation for Graduate School Admission

In this chapter, you will follow six steps to draft a LOR recommending a prospective student to a particular graduate school.

STEP 1: Collect Information on Your Prospective Student.

While this exercise may feel silly, it will help you prepare for the next time a former student asks you to write a LOR on their behalf. You may consider creating a simple template such as the following to gather pertinent details to inform your writing. For the sake of the fictional LOR you will draft for this course, either pick a friend whom you know well enough to interview, or invent an imaginary student with glowing credentials.

Name: _____

Major/Program of Study: _____

Graduation Year: _____

GPA: _____

Course(s) with the Student Enrolled:_____

Student's Rank among All Former Students:

_____ Top 5% _____ Top 10% _____ Top 25% _____ Top 50%

Description of Student's Scholarly Potential: _____

Title of Paper, Presentation, or Final Project/Thesis: _____

Description of Student's Personality and Character:_____

Modal usage

Because they are a closed set, central modals lend themselves easily to corpus-based investigation (given that simple searches with concordance software can produce clear frequency counts). Modal verbs are one of the major grammatical devices that a writer/speaker uses to convey stance. They are often used to hedge or reassert confidence in a writer's commitment to an idea or mark the level of certainty in a statement (Biber et al., 1999). As hedges, they have both epistemic (i.e., knowledge or validity) and affective (i.e., emotional) functions in suggesting probability or mitigating potential damage of critical comments (Hyland, 1998).

Recommenders—the majority of whom are faculty members in this case—sometimes exhibit the need to mitigate potential face threats in their endorsements of students' academic aptitude (see Brown & Levinson, 1987). This becomes particularly clear in the use of certain modals, primarily those of possibility or necessity, to hedge their statements regarding a student's ability or potential. On the reverse side, a faculty member who is confident in the applicant's ability can use modals to reinforce the confidence in that student's ability to contribute to and thrive in an academic environment.

When examining the LOR corpus, we saw certain patterns emerge around the usage of modals. The modals of prediction were most prevalent (e.g., "will" and "would"). This trend conforms to the understood purpose of LORs as a means of assuring evaluators about applicants' chances of success. With a vested interest in the acceptance of the student, recommenders are more likely to express confidence in their statements about the student's performance in a graduate program. The following are examples of the usage of the prediction modal "will":

1. *"I am confident that they will quickly establish themselves as an excellent teacher at both the undergraduate and graduate level."*
2. *"In recommending [Name] to your attention, I have no reservations, and I am certain you will find them a promising and avid learner."*
3. *"I feel confident that [Name] will be a diligent and productive participant in our graduate student community [in the humanities] and undoubtedly a valuable teaching assistant."*
4. *"Without a doubt, I believe that [Name] will be successful in whatever graduate program they end up attending."*

5. *"[Name] has the intellectual ability, diverse interests, personality, and drive to make an outstanding teacher of literature, one who will undoubtedly inspire their students to broaden their cultural perspectives."*

In looking at these five examples, certain patterns become clear. Every example of this usage of the modal "will" occurs near some reference to the level of confidence the writer has in the applicant. This assurance can be expressed through a direct reference to confidence or certainty or by pointing out to the reader that there are "no doubts" in these statements. In examples 1 and 2, the writer directly references this idea by stating explicitly that they are "confident" or "certain" of how the other educational institution "will" find the applicant. This "bald on-record" strategy (Brown & Levinson, 1987, p. 94) not only lets the reader know directly that the writer has confidence in the student, but by expressing it in the "I am *confident/certain*" frame, it also shows a high level of commitment. In other words, modals are not used to hedge predictions in these first two examples; instead, we have explicit statements of the writer's state of mind in regard to the applicant's teaching and learning qualities.

Examples 3, 4, and 5 refer to doubt, or rather the lack thereof. By using such enhancers as "undoubtedly" or "without a doubt," the recommenders hope to convey their strong conviction by asking the reader to trust in their judgments about the applicant. Such a pattern of use brings a certain tone of finality to the discourse between reader and writer. However, note the distinction between "feeling" confident (as in example 3) and "being" confident. The statement of "feeling" confident could perhaps be interpreted as a type of quality hedge where the writer does not endeavor to take responsibility for their statement, unlike the statement of "being," which equates confidence more with the writer's own self.

TASK EIGHTEEN: Whom Would You Interview?

Look over the first five examples of the prediction modal "will." Rank order the choices (1, for top candidate, to 5, the least qualified), using these statements as your only guide to determine who sounds most promising to interview for the opportunity (e.g., graduate admission, fellowship/grant, or faculty position).

____   I am confident that they will quickly establish themselves as an excellent teacher at
____   both the undergraduate and graduate level.

____   In recommending [Name] to your attention, I have no reservations, and I am certain
         you will find them a promising and avid learner.

____   I feel confident that [Name] will be a diligent and productive participant in our pro-
         gram and undoubtedly a valuable teaching assistant.

____   Without a doubt, I believe that [Name] will be successful in whatever graduate pro-
         gram they end up attending.

____   [Name] has the intellectual ability, diverse interests, personality, and drive to make an
         outstanding teacher of literature, one who will undoubtedly inspire their students to
         broaden their cultural perspectives.

What subtle nuances of language influence your perceptions of the individuals being
described?

_____

_____

_____

PUTTING IT INTO PRACTICE: Letter of Recommendation for Graduate School Admission

STEP 2: Draft a Narrative of Collected Information.
Concentrate on the student's intellectual aptitudes, academic credentials, and potential
for success in graduate school, and fashion a compelling story from these details. Strive
for two paragraphs of three to five sentences each.

Continuing the examination of modals of prediction, below are
some examples of the usage of the modal "would":

1. *"Overall, I would rate them certainly in the top 10 percent of our students, perhaps in the top 5 percent."*

2. *"If I had to choose one student I feel I will remember in ten years, [Name] would be that student."*

3. *"Among the roughly forty graduate students I've taught at [University], I would place [Name] in my top five, in terms of overall intellectual achievement, and in my top two in terms of literary, research and argumentative skills."*

4. *"I would rank them one of the top two students that I have taught during this past decade."*

As the examples indicate, "would" collocates more closely with indications of numerical rank than "will" and does not collocate as closely with explicit references to certainty or confidence. Expression of supposed rank of the applicant in regard to other applicants brings about the possibility of the phenomenon of inflation in LORs, where a writer exaggerates the abilities or achievements of applicants in order to give them a better chance at gaining acceptance to the institution (see Miller & Van Rybroek, 1988; Ryan & Martinson, 2000). The collocation of the word "would" with the different expressions of rank indicates a willingness to ascribe a quantitative number or category to an applicant. The level of confidence the writer has in the applicant is, in these cases, supported by the statistical data provided by the writer.

PUTTING IT INTO PRACTICE: Letter of Recommendation for Graduate School Admission

STEP 3: Write the Introduction.
   a. Develop a hook for the opening paragraph.
   b. Avoid "I am writing to . . . ."
   c. Write two or three sentences, without referring much to yourself.

Moving on from the modals of prediction, we discuss the modals of possibility: "can," "could," "may," and "might." These modals occur numerous times across the corpus, making up a much smaller percentage of the modals used. Here are two examples of the use of "can" and "could":

1. *"On the whole, I think they could be as good a doctoral student as many in the program right now."*
2. *"I believe that they could do equally solid work at the doctoral level."*

While these examples are still supportive, they can be considered instances of faint praise or "apparent commendation" (Trix & Psenka, 2003), praise that is *less* positive than the previous examples involving modals of prediction. Here we no longer see the references to a level of certainty, but instead we have collocates that involve "thinking" or "believing," verbs that also serve as another type of hedge. While the modals of prediction are often accompanied by opinions stated as if they were facts, these examples with modals of possibility are presented as opinions to be shared. This lets the reader know that the writer believes these claims to be true but does not offer up the same level of personal commitment found in the use of modals of prediction.

In addition to the lack of stated confidence, these modals are usually located near words that could be described as markers of adequacy as opposed to excellence. As previously defined, markers of adequacy indicate reaching a standard without implying a surpassing of that standard. In example 1 immediately above, the writer thinks that the referenced applicant is "as good as" other graduate students. This may seem like praise for the applicant, but the applicant is only being equated to other students without being placed in a category above them. In other words, the nature of the statement speaks of an "average" competency— not a particularly high mark of praise in a genre where most applicants often turn out to be well "above average" (Liberman, 2010). Example 2 above gives the impression of a state of stasis on the part of the applicant. The recommender considers the applicant's work "solid," a positive adjective that could pale in comparison with the many markers of excellence often found in LORs. The implicature is that the student is merely satisfactory.

Finally, if modals in LORs are arranged in a hierarchy of confidence implicature, then modals of necessity ("must" and "should") may represent the lowest level of that confidence. These modals are used most often to hedge statements about an applicant's future actions to protect the writer's face needs, as in the following extracts:

1. *"They should be able to function at your school and would be a great research assistant."*
2. *"Their maturity and self-motivation should also be assets in a doctoral program."*
3. *"As [Name] continues to reflect and grow as a teacher and scholar, they should become even better."*

In looking at these examples, we can see the evidence of hedging on the part of the writer. Example 1 immediately above paints the picture of a student who may or may not "be able to function" at the reader's school. Even though the applicant *would* be a great research assistant, this positive conclusion is dependent on the outcome of whether the student is able to *function* at the intended institution. Reading between the lines, perhaps the applicant has experienced a previous problem with transitions from one environment to another that the writer is aware of but chooses not to disclose—in other words, what is said here could be less important than what is implied. Example 3 immediately above concerns a beginning teacher who is just starting out in their career. The recommender uses the brief window of past performance as a prediction that this growth *should* continue. Instead of committing to the certainty or near-certainty of this development, the writer merely suggests that history supports the idea of this growth continuing, which is a less personal investment on the confidence scale.

TASK NINETEEN: Modal Usage in LORs

Of the modal verbs listed just below this line, which verbs fit best in the provided blanks?

can, could, may, might, must, have to, shall, should, will, would

- If I were to pick the top student in the past decade, Avram _____ have to be that person.
- I may not be the best judge of Junpei's ability at quantitative analysis; my colleague Dr. Addams _____ elaborate further on his Honors thesis project.
- My perception of Oksana's teaching acumen _____ be biased by having read her glowing course evaluations.
- To further illustrate Devante's stellar qualifications, I _____ probably relate the story of his first week in my seminar course for seniors.
- I probably _____ not divulge this fact, but I need to admit that Corinne has been my favorite TA during my tenure at this college.

It is clear from the discussion here that "will" is used with positive semantic prosodies (i.e., the manner in which presumably neutral words can change their coloring through association) and that these prosodies tend to get more neutral and more negative as the frequency of the modals analyzed goes down. As a concept, the term "semantic prosody" arises from the "phraseological" tradition of corpus linguistics associated with the focus on the typical behavior of individual lexical items in their context. The notion of negative and positive evaluation, however, as Susan Hunston (2007) argues, may be oversimplistic, since the attitudinal meaning of a word could be altered by its co-text. In other words, it might be more useful to conceptualize "semantic prosody [as] a discourse function of a sequence rather than a property of a word" (Hunston, 2007, p. 258).

The alternative terms "semantic preference" or "attitudinal preference" are suggested as perhaps better ways to refer to "frequent co-occurrence of a lexical item with items expressing a particular evaluative meaning of a lexical item" (Hunston, 2007, p. 266).

PUTTING IT INTO PRACTICE: Letter of Recommendation for Graduate School Admission

STEP 4: Describe the Individual.
   a. For the final paragraph, imagine that you are talking on the phone with the recipient of the letter.
   b. While not adopting an informal register per se, write down what you might say if you had prefaced the comments this way: "Beyond academic credentials, let me tell you about _____ as a person." Whatever you would likely brainstorm to fit in that final paragraph should go here.
   c. These personal asides should be both honest and persuasive. Your obligation is to both the recipient and the student whom you are ostensibly recommending to the university in question.

Accentuating the Positive

Now we turn to examining in more detail some of the content words and positive orientation adjectives that were attested in the lexical profile of the corpus. As previously explained, these words were divided into two categories: markers of excellence and markers of adequacy. The following are some illustrative examples of both categories:

1. *"In fact, their scores were quite extraordinary: on all eight graded exercises in the two courses, they earned A's. Please understand that I am a virulent opponent of grade inflation."*
2. *"I give [Name] my highest recommendation for admission into a doctoral program because their scholarship is exceptional, and their teaching is extraordinary."*

The word "extraordinary" in example 1 immediately above means exactly that: The applicant did something that by the writer's exacting standards was not merely ordinary. The adverbial modifier "quite" serves as a type of vague hedging, but perhaps it does not have a strong impact because of the standout quality of the adjective used. Interestingly, the writer here seems keen on raising their own credibility as well as that of the applicant. They manage to cater to their own positive self-image while letting the reader know that the applicant's accomplishments were atypical of other students and thus noteworthy. Example 2 immediately above employs both the chosen example word "extraordinary" as well as another word from the same category: "exceptional." If this student is "exceptional," then that means they surpass the normal scholarship of their peers. The two markers of excellence in such a short space combine to "intensify the force" and "sharpen the focus" (see Martin & White, 2005, p. 38). Other similar words attested in the corpus that belong to this category include "superb," "outstanding," "superior," "excellent," "best," and "finest."

Now, on the medium end of the praise spectrum, the corpus contains a few other words that also serve positive evaluation but arguably for a lesser degree. To distinguish them from the first category, these are grouped together as markers of adequacy and include such words as "good," "fine," "solid," "competent," "satisfactory," and, of course, the adjective "adequate" itself. This appraisal category may bear some superficial similarities to what Trix and Psenka (2003, p. 207) term "grindstone adjectives" (e.g., "hardworking," "dependable," "industrious," etc.) except that markers of adequacy as defined here do not necessarily focus on diligence and dependability. The following examples offer some contextual illustration (emphasis added):

1. *"They are a* good *public speaker and a* competent *teacher."*
2. *"They did* solid *work in that class and ended up getting a B+."*
3. *"[Name's] written work was pretty* good.*"*

The generic adjective "good" can be used to qualify a range of domains, as it is inarguably positive in its semantic content. However, when we consider again the paradigmatic dimension of evaluative adjectives available to LOR writers and attested in the corpus, the use of "good" does not equal the more desirable levels of skill or ability signaled by markers of excellence. There is nothing inherently negative about words such as "good," "competent," "solid," "fine," and other such adjectives, but when examined in relation to the possible words commonly used to describe applicants in this genre, these restrained descriptors suddenly appear less laudatory. The effect, of course, depends mainly upon readers' conceptions of these words and their subjective reactions, but we argue that it is also conditioned by the overall presence of more lavish praise markers. In the context of the usually celebratory tone particular to the LOR genre, the interpretation of markers of adequacy is likely to be that of an evaluation that is more "critical." Interestingly, many words in this category also tend to be preceded by adverbial modifiers such as "pretty," "somewhat," etc. (see example 3 immediately above), which can diminish their pragmatic force and weaken their positive effect even more.

PUTTING IT INTO PRACTICE: Letter of Recommendation for Graduate School Admission

STEP 5: Reach Closure.
   a. Complete the final sentence with an offer to talk by email, telephone, or video conference should the recipient require further clarification.
   b. While some boilerplate terminology can be expected, avoid coming across as if you are borrowing the "business-speak" of corporate America. For instance, you need not use the common phrases "at your earliest convenience" or "do not hesitate to contact me."
   c. Proofread the resulting draft carefully. Think of how a single mistake may reflect negatively on the applicant who asked you to recommend them.

Downplaying the Negative

Because of the subtle nature of doubt casting and negative expression, we used close reading as a necessary complement to the corpus analysis. Guided using modals of possibility and necessity as well as markers of adequacy discussed above, we further examined the letters to identify any statements of (potentially) negative information. All the identified statements were then selected and coded for their common frames.

Notably, apart from one letter, every single negatively coded LOR is also shorter than the total average word count. From a quantitative point of view, the length of letters, it seems, could serve as a good indicator/predictor of the applicant's quality and the recommender's high confidence. Most strikingly, the identified negative statements are almost always bookended by mitigation strategies. Only two instances of potentially negative presentation were found to stand on their own in one letter as two independent statements:

- *"[Name] seems a bit unsure of the direction they want to take. I also did have some report that their work as a research assistant was not always done on time."*

While there are a total of eight letters in the corpus that contain two or more instances of negative information, it is rare that a recommender will offer up two negative remarks consecutively with no intervening mitigation. The previous excerpt contains some of the most damning commentary in any of the LORs reviewed. It calls into question the applicant's sense of academic direction as well as their time management skills (notice the multiple hedges: "seems" and "a bit"). In a following short paragraph, the recommender mentions some non-specific positive traits and concludes the letter by stating that:

- *"[Name] possesses traits that are worthy of acceptance into your program. I recommend them to your Ph.D. program."*

The ending to this short and weak letter, while still commendatory, is also telling in what it does not contain. Note the absence of the usual collocates or enhancers of "recommend," such as "I *strongly, highly,* or *wholeheartedly* recommend" or "I recommend *without reservation*." Clearly, the applicant here does not have the recommender's full support.

The other remaining negative instances are presented in a formulaic way: The negative information is adjacently paired with a positive or mitigating statement. This discursive strategy seeks to get credit for honest appraisal of the applicant's qualifications while at the same time softening the potentially negative impact. The common formulas or discursive frames of combining negative and positive presentations that evolved from the data analysis are summarized in Table 4.

Table 4: Summary of Five Major Discursive Frames of Negative/Positive Pairings in LOR Corpus

Frame	Example
Frame I Subordinator + "Good," "Bad" (or Subordinator + "Bad," "Good")	Frame I *While the idea is an intriguing one, [Student 1] did not always, in these papers, provide close readings that fully substantiated their claims.*

(Continued)

Table 4: (Cont.)

Frame	Example
Frame II Specific "*Good*" in contrast to the unspecified "*Bad*"	Frame II *I will say that [Student 2's] stellar GRE scores impressed us all, although there was some skepticism about other elements of their application.*
Frame III Initially "*Bad*." "However" applicant undergoes transformation = "*Good*"	Frame III *During this semester, they rarely spoke, handed in at least one paper late, and, although clearly bright, was generally an unremarkable student. After two years of teaching in a local middle school, however, [Student 3] returned to apply to [Student 3's school] program with a new sense of commitment and intellectual curiosity.*
Frame IV "*Good,*" but "*Bad*" or "*Bad,*" but "*Good*"	Frame IV *I found them intelligent and outgoing, but their work proved to be less than first-rate.*
Frame V Like "*them,*" not particularly Good	Frame V *[Student 5] like almost all of our students was not able to have a perfect "A" record.*

Frame I

Subordinator + "*Good*", "*Bad*" or Subordinator + "*Bad,*" "*Good*"

1. *"While the idea is an intriguing one, [Name] did not always, in these papers, provide close readings that fully substantiated their claims."*
2. *"While there are certainly areas in which they need to grow as a scholar, I have been impressed by their effort."*

The first example presents the reader with positive information followed by a rather cautious presentation of negative information. The phrases "not always" and "in these papers" aim to give some context to indicate that the writer is referring to very specific incidents, but perhaps the applicant has the ability to perform close reading in other assignments. The second example presents the negative information first and foregrounds the "honesty" concern that has been discussed in other studies (Aamodt & Bryan, 1993). In this example, a legitimate concern is presented, followed by a positive assessment in a vague area ("effort") in which the applicant is supposedly "impressive" and does not "need to grow as a scholar." "Effort," however, seems to be one of those "code" words that can be taken to mean "the student is trying but they are certainly not trying hard enough."

Frame II

Specific *"Good"* in contrast to the unspecified *"Bad"*

- *"I will say that [Name's] stellar GRE scores impressed us all, although there was some skepticism about other elements of their application."*

The example of this formula makes use of two of what could be described as "standout" words: "stellar" and "impress" (see Schmader et al., 2007, p. 514). This positive presentation is followed by a contrastive word, which signifies a shift in thought. The negative information is then presented, but it should be noted that the writer—unlike the specific mention of GRE scores—does not go into detail about these "other elements" in the application package. This lack of specificity may defuse the impact of the negative presentation, but then again it may exacerbate it for some readers.

Frame III

Initially *"Bad."* "However," undergoes transformation = *"Good"*

1. *"During this semester, they rarely spoke, handed in at least one paper late, and, although clearly bright, was generally an unremarkable student. After two years of teaching in a local middle school, however, [Name] returned to apply to [Named University] program with a new sense of commitment and intellectual curiosity."*
2. *"Initially a bit shy, they developed confidence over the two semesters as demonstrated through improved class participation."*

The formula involving the applicant's undergoing some form of personal or professional transformation, as we can see from both examples above, often relates to public persona or shyness. In fields where the applicants are often required to present their own opinions verbally and support them in front of a room full of people, as is the case with the humanities and education, an applicant's reticence could be perceived as a negative factor. The transformation is the result of experience gained in a teaching position (in the first example) or time (in the second example) that helped the applicant to overcome this perceived shortcoming.

TASK TWENTY: Coding Potentially Negative Information

If you were serving on a graduate school admissions committee, what would give you pause in the sections labeled in this chapter as Frames I–III? Isolate the potentially problematic line(s), writing a brief justification for what alarms or concerns you about the statement(s) you choose to highlight.

Frame IV

"Good," but *"Bad"* or *"Bad,"* but *"Good"*

1. *"I found them intelligent and outgoing, but their work proved to be less than first-rate."*
2. *"They are not absolutely the brightest graduate student I've known, but they are one of the brightest, and their writing has always demonstrated more intellectual curiosity and a little more ambition than is the norm here."*

The interpretation of the word "but" will always create the conventional implicature of a sense of contrast; almost half the examples of negative/positive pairing depend on this common frame. The last two examples give us a view of the more basic means of pairing positive information with negative information. One set of information is stated, then the other is offered as a counterpoint either for downgrading or upgrading. The statements here differ from the examples of Frames I and II primarily in their consistent use of the coordinating conjunction "but." Example 1 immediately above operates on the basis that while the qualities initially presented are considered valuable in an academic community, the institution being applied to supposedly wants its applicants to be of a higher quality. Note that in this example, we have another hedge, which is the avoidance of the direct expression of the negative. The circumlocutory choice of "less than first-rate" is clearly a euphemism for "inadequate" or at least "not good enough." This semantic point illustrates the wide range of possible linguistic resources for delivering negative evaluation and the potential insufficiency of corpus methods alone in capturing language nuances.

Speaking of semantics, the second example presents a case of ambiguity regarding the use of the word "absolutely." Does the writer intend this sentence to be read as "They are not the [absolute] brightest graduate student I have ever known" or "They are [absolutely] not the brightest graduate student I have ever known"? The actual intentions of the writer may not matter in the reader's reception of the sentence. The reader is going to perceive this sentence one way or the other, but the polarity effect of "not" (to use Martin and White's terms) is still potentially negative. The recommender, however, does rank the student higher "than is the norm here" in the areas of ambition and intellectual curiosity.

TASK TWENTY-ONE: Understanding Discursive Frames

To demonstrate that you understand the discursive frames outlined in Table 4, compose your own examples of each pairing of positive and negative traits for a fictional applicant.

FRAME I

Subordinator + "Good," "Bad" (or Subordinator + "Bad," "Good")

_____

_____

FRAME II

Specific "Good" in contrast to the unspecified "Bad"

_____

_____

FRAME III

Initially "Bad." "However," applicant undergoes transformation = "Good"

_____

_____

FRAME IV

"Good," but *"Bad"* or *"Bad,"* but *"Good"*

_____

_____

_____

PUTTING IT INTO PRACTICE: Letter of Recommendation for Graduate School Admission

STEP 6: Write the Accompanying Email or Complete the Survey.

> Generally, these LORs are uploaded through a dossier service, the university's website (via a provided link), or by email. Certain universities require recommenders to complete a simple survey about the applicant using Likert scales or banks of character qualities to check. For this assignment, imagine that you have been asked to send an email with the LOR as an attachment. Compose a brief yet professional email to the Director of Graduate Admissions at the fictional university for which you are recommending this applicant.

Frame V

Like "them," *not particularly Good*

There are two instances of the potentially negative being presented in a different but still formulaic fashion, given below.

1. *"Like most of the students in the "Educational leadership" course, they came to it with little or no knowledge of assessment and testing."*
2. *"[Name], like almost all of our students, was not able to have a perfect 'A' record."*

The potentially negative is presented here without any explicit positive information. Instead, it is paired with an excuse to avoid singling out the student. In both examples, the excuse is that the applicant exhibits some type of academic limitation, but so do their peers. The perceived weakness, therefore, is somewhat ameliorated. Although unsaid, example 1 above does imply that even though the student initially had no knowledge of the subject matter when they "came" to the class, they departed with the required knowledge that they previously lacked.

TASK TWENTY-TWO: Writing the LOR for Graduate Admission

NOTE: *The following genre text type is not intended to serve as a template for future letters. Rather, this example uses the best practices of our research into the LOR subgenre of graduate school admission.*

Complete the sample Admissions LOR for a student applying to a PhD program. Keep in mind that this applicant uses she/her personal pronouns. Feel free to make up any details to fill in the provided blanks.

Dear Professor _____,

It is my pleasure to recommend [Name] for admission to the _____ program at [Named University]. She currently works as _____ and has recently decided to pursue her PhD in_____. In fall of _____, she took my course _____, where she received a well-deserved A in the class. My understanding is that she is primarily interested in anthropology and her interest in my class was a result of her curiosity about sociocultural variation. She eventually hopes to teach anthropology at the collegiate level.

I do remember [Name] as someone who illustrated a consistent ability to work independently as well as collaboratively. She was friendly, collegial, well-organized, hardworking, and active in class discussions. In short, she possesses traits that are worthy of acceptance into your program; in fact, she is someone who would[1] be an asset to any department, and I recommend her admission wholeheartedly and without any reservation.[2]

Thank you for considering my recommendation and [Name's] application. If you have any questions about the student's qualifications you think I might be able to address, please do not hesitate to contact me. The easiest way to reach me is by email; my address is listed above.

Sincerely,
[Recommender's name and institutional affiliation]

On a Lighter Note

The British philosopher Paul Grice (1975) gives the following famous example about a notoriously brief reference letter written for a graduate student of philosophy. The recommender's letter simply reads:

"Dear Sir, Mr. X's command of English is excellent, and his attendance at tutorials has been regular. Yours, name."

The letter clearly flouts what Grice calls the Maxim of Quantity (i.e., the unspoken expectation to make one's contribution as informative as is required for the current purposes of the exchange). In a high-stakes rhetorical situation where elaboration is expected, brevity can be the soul of doubt!

In reading such a dubiously brief letter, the thought process of the letter readers might go something like this: The applicant is the recommender's student, so the recommender cannot be unable, through ignorance, to add more information. If the recommender wished to be uncooperative, why bother to write the letter at all? The only plausible inference, then, is that the recommender might be wishing to implicitly convey information that he is reluctant to explicitly put down on paper. Mr. X must be a terrible student who is not at all good at philosophy! What is not explicitly stated can be as salient as (or even more salient than) what is. LORs, for better or for worse, are telling in both commission and omission.

It seems intuitive that if we like something, we tend to invest more time and effort in it than we do with something we don't like. Albert Mehrabian (1965) found subjects wrote longer recommendation letters for someone they liked rather than someone they disliked. And letter readers seem to share the same sentiment, and thus a short evaluation is less likely to make as much positive impression on them as a longer one. In other words, we can say that there is quality in quantity, something that we also encounter in product reviews.

Based on data drawn from thousands of reviews at *Wine Enthusiast* magazine, a study by Mark Liberman (2012) concluded that the length of wine reviews measured in words was a major factor in the numerical rating given to the associated wine. At least 25 percent of the variance in ratings can be explained by the length of the review alone. Perhaps "brief" is not always to the point, and "short" is not always sweet.

Conclusion

The problem of interpreting recommendations is that some LOR writers tend to be superlative, while others are more reserved. This can complicate candidate calibration, but it does not necessarily get in the way of successful communication (Liberman, 2010). Moreover, the interpretation of any remarks in LORs is conditioned not only by the context of reception and readers' subjectivity but also by the readers' experience with the conventions of the genre. By their very nature, though, LORs tend to have a "superiority bias"; in other words, they tend to overstate positive qualities and understate negative ones. While this awareness should be taken as an element in the evaluative considerations we apply to these texts, it may also lead us to judge them according to an unfairly higher standard (see Miller & Van Rybroek, 1988). Paradoxically, in a genre where most applicants receive "wholehearted" and "enthusiastic" recommendations, even words and comments that normally present positive information can be seen negatively in the company of other more glowing letters in the same group.

Discussion Questions

1. Which hedges are you most apt to use? Why do these linguistic constructions come more naturally to you than others? Try rephrasing a potential LOR scenario using hedges that are more unfamiliar to you. How do these specific hedging choices affect the inherent rhetorical message?
2. When might subtly negative language creep into a description in an LOR, influencing a reader's perception of the applicant? How might you, as the recommender, mitigate any unintended interpretations while still raising legitimate concerns about the person in question?
3. How might you as an LOR writer avoid inflating the credentials or competence of the person you are recommending? What might occur if you overpromise how praiseworthy a given candidate might be?

Instructor Suggestions

If you have not already brought up the controversial nature of LORs and the clamor within some ranks of academia to replace them with surveys that use Likert scales, which would rate applicants between 1 and 5 on certain measures, now would be a good time to introduce this debate. Assigning two short readings that represent the opposing views on the matter could be illustrative for students.

Reading on the positive side, supporting LORs in academia:

Albakry, M. (2022, December 5). On writing and decoding recommendation letters. *Inside Higher Ed.* https://www.insideh ighered.com/advice/2022/12/06/advice-junior-faculty-writing-rec ommendation-letters-opinion

Reading on the more negative side, questioning the validity of some academic LORs:

Antonacci, P. (2020, November 9). Reference letters in academic admissions: Useful or useless? *Acuity Insights.* https://acuityinsig hts.com/admissions/reference-letters-academic-admissions-use ful-useless/

One pedagogical option: Ask students to conduct a mini debate, raising the points posited in each article. Follow up by asking how the sponsoring website may help to reinforce the claims made by each author.

Notes

1. Notice the use of the more assertive modal "would" rather than using more probabilistic modals such as "could," for example.
2. One of the formulaic expressions that usually appears at the end of an LOR to signal full endorsement.

CHAPTER 7

Phrase Frames and Customary Closings

Sample LOR

The following excerpt, drawn from an actual LOR submitted by a colleague on behalf of a job applicant for an academic position, demonstrates the principles and rhetorical practices outlined in this chapter. Read it over to gain a sense of how this microgenre operates.

> *Although I kept adding responsibilities to their portfolio, Dr. [Name] received and executed them diligently and in a timely manner. They are an excellent resource person and apply intellectual rigor to everything they embark upon. I was highly impressed with, among other things, their willingness to do extensive research on ideas before submitting well thought-out proposals, with due consideration for contextualizing best practices. Their work on the consolidated institution's promotion and tenure policies, the Chair policy, curriculum revision, and the faculty support through the Center for Teaching Excellence exemplified this approach of deliberation and thoughtfulness.*
>
> *Dr. [Name] has shown an astute ability to navigate challenging personalities and situations as evident in their work with the faculty senate on the promotion and tenure policy for the new institution, as well as their work on the Consolidation Implementation Committee on preserving the history of the two institutions as they transitioned into one. Dr. [Name]'s leadership style is collegial and exemplifies a servant-leader philosophy.*

They can match big picture with faculty-level and student-level practice.
I have the utmost confidence in Dr. [Name]'s ability to lead in a chair's
position, and I gladly recommend them for your consideration.

Please let me know if I can be of further help in your consideration of
Dr. [Name]'s candidacy.

Sincerely,

Overview

While much of this book has focused on the rhetorical moves and linguistic features of the LOR, certain aspects of formal correspondence also apply when writing such a professional referral on someone's behalf. Writing a standard business letter requires the writer to abide by certain required conventions: a date; the inside address of the recipient; a salutation with the appropriate title (e.g., Mr., Ms., or Dr.), followed by a colon; the body of the letter; an appropriate closing or sign-off (e.g., "Sincerely" or "Best regards"); and a signature, along with the title of the sender and an indication of enclosures (if applicable). Moreover, professional correspondence favors block format (viz., flush left margins) with a blank line between paragraphs. Even something as individualized as realizing that most business letters rarely stretch beyond a single page—unless the writer must answer specific prompts for the rhetorical situation—is of great importance.

With such a formal structure in mind, the unfamiliar writer also may unconsciously import into their writing other aspects commonly seen in other letters, thinking them to be requirements. For instance, opening the letter the way many writers do with the phrase "I am writing to . . ." allows the correspondent to announce the purpose straightaway, but the customary move lacks elegance and may inadvertently work against their stated purpose of making a convincing case to consider the individual merits of the person being recommended. Similarly, many letters close with some variation of the following phrase: "Please do not hesitate to contact me . . . ." While understandable, this gracious move loses some of its rhetorical force by its sheer overuse.

This chapter explores the appearance of so-called "boilerplate language" in actual LORs, analyzing where in the letter writers tend to resort to commonplace phrases, perhaps to legitimize the LOR as belonging to the genre and help the recipient to recognize it for its rhetorical aim. We will also see together how various recommenders endeavor to convey the purpose of the letter. The sheer variety of actual moves demonstrates that some writers prefer to launch immediately into the promotional genre, explicitly stating the aim of the LOR. Conversely, others prefer to soften their approach with an affective move, appealing to the emotions of the recipient through careful word choice. Finally, nearly all writers we have encountered follow certain formulas in beginning and ending their letters to leave a lasting positive impression of the colleague whom they wish to refer for the opportunity in question.

A Teaching Example

In the following example, taken from the final two paragraphs of an LOR written on behalf of an academic job candidate, the writer sums up their appreciation of the applicant's merits, ending with a last sentence that follows several standard conventions while riffing on the customary closing of a piece of professional correspondence.

> It should come as no surprise then that I give [Name] my highest and most enthusiastic recommendation. They are, quite simply, one of the best teachers I have ever seen, whether in conventional classes or innovative ones. I have no doubt that they will continue to challenge . . . their students to reach for the highest possible success. . . . In addition, they are a wonderful colleague and collaborator, and will contribute much to any academic or professional environment.
>
> If can be of any further assistance in your decision-making process, please do not hesitate to contact me, either by email at [redacted] or on my cell phone at [redacted].

To the instructor: In your classroom, ask students to repeat the phrases that they have heard elsewhere in this book or in other professional letters. If these phrases are so familiar, why do they suppose writers employ them intentionally? Conversely, what unique additions to the customary closing does this writer include? What messages may be inferred from them?

TASK TWENTY-THREE: Considering Business Letters

Even in the age of email, people's mailboxes fill up with actual printed business correspondence daily in the form of bills, appeals from charities, offers to purchase something, etc. The tone and diction (what linguists prefer to call "register") can be labeled "formal," as opposed to the informality of a handwritten birthday card or text from a friend or loved one. Because these types of standard letters are so familiar, we may not examine them closely to understand how their parts fit together to represent a bona fide example of a business letter. Do you know the various sections of a professional letter?

In this activity, label the parts of the letter using the key below the example. *Note: This letter does not fit the genre of a recommendation.*

Ima Student

0000 Main Street, Apt. 0
Bryan, WA 000$0
Email: ima.student@internet.com

February 27, 202__

Registrar's Office
University of Springfield
1234 College Way
Springfield, WA 00000

RE: Transcript request for Student, I.

Dear Registrar's office personnel:

In applying to a doctoral program at Burke University, I need to supply transcripts from my undergraduate program in Educational Studies (minor in TESOL) from the University of Springfield.

I was enrolled at the Springfield campus from 2018–2022. I graduated in May 2022. If it helps to locate my records, my student number was 12345678.

Thank you for sending me five copies of the printed transcript; my address is listed above. I have enclosed a check to cover the fee.

Sincerely,

Ima Student
Ima R. Student

Enclosure: check #1376

The following parts of a business letter are not given in chronological order. Feel free to consult the Internet (if you must) to become more familiar with the conventions of a professional letter. Use this list to label the parts of the letter.

- Body paragraphs
- Closing or conclusion
- Complimentary close
- Date
- Enclosures (optional)
- Greeting/salutation
- Heading/letterhead
- Opening
- Reference
- Signature and writer's identification
- Subject
- The inside address

Why the Customary Opening Is Lackluster

In first-year writing courses on college campuses, students are often taught the time-tested technique of opening an essay with a "hook," a riveting statistic or anecdote that acts as a "compelling lead," inviting the interested reader to explore the text further (Rief, 2019, p. 31). An interesting LOR should stand out from the rest without sounding gimmicky or outlandish in tone. Some recommenders begin their letter to an anonymous review committee by employing customary openings that reflect "'institutionalized expressions' functioning as 'bookends' to the text" (Nattinger & DeCarrico, 1992, p. 39). Certain greetings reflect the standard conventions of business correspondence—with or without salutations. Fully half of the LORs contain no salutation. Of the twenty attested salutations, various options exist—from generalized to specific. The bulk use a greeting geared toward this specific rhetorical situation (viz., "To the Review Committee"); a general salutation (e.g., "To Whom It May Concern"); and a dated greeting ("Dear Sir or Madam") as well as a potentially problematic opening ("Dear Sirs").

Despite the lack of salutation, the LORs nonetheless still open effectively by using deictic framing that overtly labels the textual content that follows. Explicitly stating the communicative purpose of the letter (reifying the move) comes in a portion of the letters via the multi-word expression (MWE) customary in business correspondence: "I am writing to*" in different variations:

- *"I am writing in support of [Name]'s application."*
- *"I am writing to provide my wholehearted support for the project submitted by Professor [Name]."*
- *"I am writing to recommend [Name] for a Residential Fellowship."*
- *"I am writing to enthusiastically recommend [Name] for your fellowship."*
- *"I am writing to support [Name]'s application for a fellowship at . . ."*

A recent article published by National Public Radio offered advice to college students applying for their limited, highly competitive internships: Stop using the customary opening "I am writing" (Drummond & Nadworny, 2017). These authors claim that most cover letters need some work—even from the first three words: "I am writing . . . ." Instead of starting so much on the nose with independent clauses such as "I am writing to express my interest" or "I am writing to apply for the internship," they suggest using a hook to make one's cover letter stand out from the stack and to ensure your résumé floats to the top of the pile of applicants. The same conditions are true with LORs. A general statement about the ideal candidate's qualifications sets up the writer to then suggest their particular applicant fits the proverbial bill.

TASK TWENTY-FOUR: Opening with a Hook

To distinguish an applicant from potential competitors, an astute LOR writer may choose to pen a general opening statement before suggesting that the individual in question fulfills these characteristics. Review the two openings below (drawn from actual LORs).

EXCERPT #1:

A brilliant mind and a humble, self-effacing personality make for a rare combination in academia today—even among undergraduate students. Far too many graduates in my recent memory seem convinced of their stellar qualities, despite their young age. Therefore, when someone stands out from the crowd by their hard work ethic, their drive, and their outstanding scholarly achievements—all while remaining modest about such accolades—they tend to make a strong impression. _____ is just such a person.

EXCERPT #2:

I am writing in support of _____ 's application for a _____ fellowship to work on their project, entitled _____.

Which excerpt gives you a more favorable impression? Why?

_____

_____

In what circumstances might a selection committee appreciate the matter-of-fact approach of excerpt #2? Why?

_____

_____

Other writers have framed their opening move by referring to having been requested to pen the recommendation:

- *"[Name] has asked me to write . . ."*
- *"I have been asked . . ."*
- *"This [letter] is to recommend . . ."*
- *"My purpose of writing is to recommend . . ."*

Having been asked by an applicant not only provides a deictic frame—namely, the resulting letter serves as the response to the request—but it also allows recommenders to gesture toward their importance within a given field. They must be fairly well-established scholars to be the types of experts called on to write recommendation letters, thereby reinforcing their ethos or credibility.

LANGUAGE FOCUS: EMOTIVE TERMS IN LORs

The openings, while conventional at times, frequently carry affective connotations. In nearly half of the LORs, the writer mentions being "pleased," as in the collocation "pleased to write," or experiencing "pleasure"—even intensified as "deep" or "great" pleasure. These writers mention their willingness to recommend, including the following collocations and lexical terms in the same semantic field: "delighted," "wholehearted," "enthusiastically," "great enthusiasm," and "strongest terms."

Some of the affective terms reappear in one of the final rhetorical moves within a typical letter, wherein the writer closes the LOR with a summative recommendation based on the individual strengths of the applicant, adding emotive words to augment their hearty endorsement of the candidate's valuation.

The recurrence of particular phrases (with minimal lexical variation), especially in the first move dedicated to sharing the purpose for the correspondence, demonstrates the rhetorical formulaicity (i.e., the condition of being formulaic and unoriginal) that many writers employ when composing opening lines of LORs (Bhatia, 2004). Below is a compilation of multi-word expressions of five-term strings within a set of fellowship-related LORs in our corpus (see Table 5), designated by the number of occurrences and the prevalent moves where they are often situated.

Table 5: Frequent Multi-Word Expressions (of Five Terms) in LOR Corpus

I * (am/ have been/ was/ became) * (very/ greatly/ particularly) impressed by	I can think of no
I am * to do so (very pleased/ delighted)	I first met * in
To Whom It May Concern	I have known * since
* in the history of	have known * for almost
to write in support of	Since then I have followed
in support of * application	of the ways in which
has asked me to write	students that I have taught
to recommend * for a	I am particularly impressed by
am very pleased to write	I am looking forward to
I am delighted to recommend	do not hesitate to contact
* work in the field (of)	

Read together, these multi-word expressions or p-frames reveal a degree of prefabricated writing that typifies a recognizable LOR, but the individual letters' word choice differs significantly enough to negate the notion that writers follow a template marked by commonplace phrasing. The individualized verbal expressions within the letters in the corpus reflect an elevated register marked by the stylistic variation one might expect from career academics.

How to Write Effective Closings

As a bounded writing genre, the LOR naturally includes ways that different writers conclude the text, indicating that they have fulfilled their communicative aim suitably. Many of these final statements indicate the desire to leave a positive impression of the respective candidate and their potential. For instance, one recommender, mentioned in the previous discussion, promises a publishing contract for the book that the applicant will finish if given the fellowship opportunity, and thus finds a unique way to end the letter on the merits of the scholarly production without writing a final line praising the candidate. These more abrupt and/or unique concluding statements are outliers. Prominently, most recommendation letters that we have encountered employ a final affirmation of the respective individual.

Summative recommendations

More than three-quarters of the recommenders—regardless of LOR type—include a final summative recommendation before signing their names. In other words, LOR writers sense the need to reiterate at the conclusion of the LOR that they indeed offer their full support of the candidate, confidence in their potential, or both. For instance, one recommender's hearty endorsement of a book project on an under-studied nineteenth- and twentieth-century historical figure ends with the following summative statement: *"You can support this work with complete confidence that you are supporting a very significant and worthwhile project."* Note the doubling of the variations on the term "support," along with the adjectives "complete," "significant" (intensified by the adverb of degree "very"), and "worthwhile."

Generally, however, the recommenders tend to focus on the person whose accomplishments and personal traits they have extolled earlier in the LOR. In the following instance, the recommender uses the word "deserve," a term suggesting the applicant's worthiness: *"I am sure [Name] deserves the support that your award of such a Fellowship will guarantee; and you can be assured of the prestigious development in your colleague."* Or *"In conclusion, I strongly endorse [Name] for the assistant professor position in education at your university. They possess the character, teaching ability, and research skills that are essential for success in your research-intensive university."* To promise full "assurance" to the review committee that the potential recipient will develop as a result seems risky, but the language indicates that the recommender counts on this applicant as a sure bet.

Of course, the summative statement does not take the place of the elaborated recommendation in the preceding paragraphs. Instead, this statement may simply be following an internalized template of sorts. When completing checklists and surveys as recommendation forms rather than narrative-based letters, often the final question asks the recommender to rate whether the recommendation is made with any reservation or hesitation. We speculate that this model of leaving a final impression of wholehearted endorsement informs this frequent step.

When to Use "Boilerplate Language"

Offering further information via standardized statements

As mentioned above, letter writers may feel inclined to conclude with examples of what we label "boilerplate terminology" p-frames that one expects to read in professional correspondence written for a corporate audience. The phrasing varies slightly from letter to letter, yet customarily reads like the following statement: "Please do not hesitate to contact me." This politeness step provides a recognized way to end the letter, even if follow-up contact remains highly unlikely.

The "hesitation" phrase is not the only means writers resort to in terms of customary business-writing phrases. While certainly making a sincere offer to clarify any written comments further if requested, one recommender completes the letter similarly: *"Please let me know if I can do anything further in support of [Name]'s application."* Perhaps the final step indicates that many recommenders internalize the notion that the LOR stands alone as a rhetorical artifact that must act solely on what's included and excluded; they do not expect to receive further correspondence.

Less common—yet significant nonetheless—is the move that expresses thanks to the review committee for considering the LOR. This rare summation should not imply that the other LORs use a curt tone, however. Clearly, recommenders infer that an overt gratitude statement is unnecessary in this conventionalized genre. The terms of the transaction— namely, writing the evaluative approbation as requested to complete the applicant's file—do not necessitate thanking the readers for upholding their part of the arrangement. Moreover, such a statement may seem a type of filler, occupying valuable word count better dedicated to lauding the candidate's credentials.

TASK TWENTY-FIVE: Look Familiar?

Which of these common phrases have you seen in professional letters? Rank order them (1 for most familiar) in order of their familiarity to you.

____ *If I can be of further help, please do not hesitate to contact me.*
____ *[Name] has asked me to write a letter on their behalf.*
____ *Please contact me at your earliest convenience.*
____ *I am writing to you today to . . .*
____ *[Name] is a real "people person."*

If these phrases seem familiar, what is the likelihood that they will also sound tired or trite to the recipient? What could be detrimental about coming across as too formulaic in one's writing?

_____

_____

_____

TASK TWENTY-SIX: Critique a Recommendation Letter

The following composite letter is written in support of a candidate who is applying for an assistant professor position in education. Do you think it is specific enough in its details? What details do you find more effective? Would you hire the person recommended?

Dear Search Committee Members:

I am writing to enthusiastically endorse [Name] for the assistant professor position in education at your [Name] university. I have had the privilege of working with [Name] for the past several years and have been consistently impressed with their teaching ability, research quality, and exceptional character traits.

One of [Name]'s most outstanding qualities is their teaching style. They have a natural talent for engaging students and creating an inclusive learning environment that fosters growth and development. [Name] is deeply committed to student learning. Their approach to teaching is characterized by a high level of enthusiasm and rigor. They use innovative teaching methods that stimulate critical thinking, and their ability to connect with students is exceptional. Students speak highly of [Name]'s teaching, citing their ability to inspire and motivate students to achieve their goals.

[Name] has a talent for making complex concepts understandable and relevant to their students. They are skilled at creating meaningful connections between course content and real-world applications, which helps their students to better understand the importance of their coursework. I know that [Name] is committed to using evidence-based teaching practices and is always seeking new strategies to enhance student learning and engagement.

Furthermore, [Name] is a highly productive and accomplished scholar. Their research is focused on [specific research area], and they have made significant contributions to the field. Their research has been published in several prestigious academic journals, and they have presented their work at numerous conferences and secured significant research funding. They are a respected member of the academic community and have a strong record of successful collaborations with other researchers in the field. Their work is highly regarded and has received national and international recognition.

On a personal level, [Name] has a great personality and their character is impeccable. They treat colleagues and students with respect and kindness, and they are always willing to lend a helping hand. Their positive attitude and energy are infectious, and they bring out the best in those around them. [Name] is a dedicated, hardworking, highly ethical, trustworthy, and conscientious individual who possesses exceptional leadership skills. They have a strong passion for education and are committed to making a difference in the lives of their students. Their work ethic and commitment to excellence are second to none, and they consistently exceed expectations in all aspects of their work.

In conclusion, [Name] is an exceptional individual who is committed to advancing knowledge and improving the lives of students. I highly recommend them for the assistant professor position in education, and I am confident that they will make valuable contributions to your institution.

Sincerely,

[Recommender's name and institutional affiliation]

The Horrors (and Promise) of AI-Generated Text

We hate to see the act of writing a personal LOR being automated in the name of saving time and increasing efficiency. The formulaic nature of some parts of the LOR, however, created an opening for organizational communication entrepreneurs (e.g., Lucinetic.com) to use generative artificial intelligence (AI) large language models (LLMs) to help craft "the perfect letter of recommendation." They market themselves to customers as being able to leverage the power of "generative AI workflow and your unique information to create personalized and impactful letters that will set you apart from your competitors and leave a lasting impression." Using the applicant's inputs and notes, the company boasts that their AI-boosted writing assistant structures a draft that can match the recommender's writing style and thus saves busy faculty from agonizing for hours about the best way to express their support in a letter. To make the letter more specific, the proprietary software lets applicants suggest topics for their writer to discuss in the letter. In other words, the AI service allows the letter writer and the applicant to work together to co-create a tailored recommendation. They also claim that the company's "ethically trained" AI-writing algorithm has been "meticulously taught by the world's top faculty, students, and DEI professionals."

Specificity and ethics, however, do not seem to be major concerns for ChatGPT (https://chat.openai.com)—a free generative AI application that has taken the world by storm since its initial release in November 2022. The application has been in circulation in the public domain for less than one year (at the time of writing), but it is already the fastest

growing application to date. Not only can ChatGPT simplify and sum-
marize texts, but it can also generate new "original" texts on command.
The chatbot boasts an impressive capacity for generating plausible-
sounding answers as well as detailed, human-like texts including essays,
responses, recipes, lyrics, and letter forms of any kind—including recommendation letters.

To test the capacity of ChatGPT, we entered the prompt "Write a
letter of recommendation for a faculty position in American history," and
in a matter of seconds, we got the following letter:

Dear Hiring Committee,

I am writing to enthusiastically recommend [Name] for the faculty
position in American history. I have had the pleasure of working with
[Name] in the field of history for several years, and I can confidently
say that they are an exceptional historian with a deep understanding of
American history.

[Name] holds a PhD in American history from [University], and
their research expertise lies in the history of [specific subfield]. Their
dissertation, which examined [topic], was a groundbreaking work that
contributed significantly to the field. Since then, [Name] has continued
to publish extensively on this topic, as well as other areas of American
history. Their research is not only of the highest quality but is also of great
relevance to contemporary issues.

[Name] is also an outstanding teacher. They have taught a wide range
of courses, including surveys of American history, upper-level seminars,
and graduate courses. Students consistently praise [Name]'s teaching
style, which is engaging, rigorous, and challenging. [Name] is also deeply
committed to mentoring students, both undergraduate and graduate, and
has successfully supervised several theses and dissertations.

In addition to their research and teaching, [Name] has been an active
member of the profession. They have presented papers at numerous
conferences, served on editorial boards, and reviewed articles for several
leading journals. They have also been involved in organizing conferences
and workshops, and their service to the profession has been recognized by
several awards and honors.

Overall, I cannot recommend [Name] highly enough for your faculty position in American history. Please do not hesitate to contact me if you require any further information.

Sincerely,

[Your Name]

The letter does not provide concrete examples or personal anecdotes, nor does it make any specific reference to the applicant's character, but it is remarkable, nonetheless, in its "human-like" text. It impressively emulates the generic template with its conventional formulaic divisions of the holy trinity of the academic's responsibilities and expectations: research, teaching, and service. But perhaps that is not surprising given that ChatGPT has reportedly been trained on a massive amount of human-written data of all genres and thus was able to reproduce a plausible amalgamation. It is possible, however, to have a more effective letter if the recommender provides personal details to make the letter more "human" and heartfelt. Rather than relying on a machine-generated text, the recommender could adopt a machine-assisted approach.

For now, AI seems very good at simulating the form more than the function, and its output is sometimes riddled with errors and factual inaccuracies. Despite its flaws, it is not unreasonable, however, given the fast pace of AI advancement, to speculate that AI may change the way we conceive of the writing process and our notion of creativity. As of the time of finishing this book, it is fair to say that the academic community is still wrestling with the ethical, legal, and philosophical implications of ChatGPT and the general impact of other AI large language models.

On a Lighter Note

For amusement, we entered another facetious prompt asking the ChatGPT to "write a letter of recommendation for a faculty position in Shakespearean studies in the style of a sonnet." Sure enough, the chatbot humored us with the following letter/sonnet, which is not exactly in uplifting or soul-stirring Shakespearean language, but at least follows the poetic form with its conventional structure and rhyme scheme.

My dearest committee members, pray, take note,
Of one whose scholarship in Shakespeare's art,
Is peerless in its scope and doth connote,
A scholar of the highest skill and heart.

My pen must sing the praises of this one,
Whose scholarly pursuits are rare and bright,
Whose knowledge of the Bard's works, so well done,
Doth fill our hearts with wonder and delight.

In truth, my friends, I cannot recommend,
[Name] too highly for this faculty post,
Their scholarship and skill shall not descend,
But rise and make your Shakespearean studies boast.
So, hear my humble sonnet, hear my plea,
And hire [Name], whose worth is plain to see.

Final Thoughts

Regardless of what they teach or research, one of faculty members' primary functions might be evaluation. Writing and reading letters of recommendation is one of the most important evaluative tasks of an academic's professorial life. The effort that goes into composing reference letters can be a time-consuming task for seasoned professors, but it can be a much more daunting one for junior faculty who may never have even seen a letter of recommendation before—including the ones sent on their own behalf when they applied for graduate schools and academic positions. Like other genres, the letter of recommendation is ever fluid, and its conventions can shift somewhat, depending on differing audiences, disciplinary expectations, and institutional contexts. Still, we can find some discernible, rather universal, patterns in its structure, content, and language—thus allowing for some general suggestions.

When a letter is written in a nuanced voice, it can be very revealing. Moreover, if we learn to be sensitive to its conventions and patterns, we can use the LOR to provide a wealth of information and insights about applicants. If you are an early-career academic, becoming more cognizant of the inner workings of those rhetorical moves and accepted structures can help you develop the facility to produce and decode the genre far more effectively.

Instructor Suggestion

Do not be surprised if this chapter raises the greatest number of questions among your students. They may have never put much thought into the rhetorical moves embedded in simple formatting choices or the unintended messages sent via boilerplate language in a business letter. Unfortunately, some graduate students and newly minted PhDs have little experience in the corporate or non-profit sector, so drafting professional correspondence may seem daunting. Consider recommending that they purchase the accessible and affordable book by Paul MacRae entitled *Business and Professional Writing: A Basic Guide—Second Edition* (2019). Despite its being a textbook, MacRae's clear writing style allows this book to function as a handy reference guide to best practices when writing for a professional audience.

Glossary

Academic Discourse: Spoken and written language used to communicate in collegiate settings or with a well-educated audience. Usually, it involves the dissemination of academic research in academic monographs and peer-reviewed journals. Some discourse types, however, are more private in nature and are not related to scholarly research dissemination (e.g., letters of recommendation and research statements).

Academic Writing: The aggregate of written genres found most often in higher education. This type of scholarly writing is part of academic work, and though the content and style may vary across genres and disciplines, it is often marked by elevated rhetorical style with fairly stable rhetorical moves, formal register, and standard written English (SWE) conventions.

Boilerplate Language: A metaphor drawn from the corporate world, this phrase describes customary phrases that appear frequently in business-related documents. They appear so often that discourse participants may no longer question their inclusion or even interrogate their meaning. In the letter of recommendation (LOR) genre, these standard phrases often open (e.g., "I am writing to you to recommend [Name] . . .") or close (e.g., "Please do not hesitate to contact me . . .") the correspondence.

Boosters: Adverbials used for positive emphasis.

Character: The composite of internalized beliefs, ethics, and cultural values that govern one's behavior; the reputation by which others know and describe an individual—particularly when recommending them for employment or consideration for admission to a competitive program. This includes a person's ethical, moral, or relational makeup and/or capacity, observable by their actions and demeanor, often articulated by a colleague in a letter of recommendation (LOR).

Disciplinary Discourse: The characteristic forms of communication unique to a respective academic discipline or major. These forms may vary in their understanding of how the discourse is organized, what counts as knowledge, and the specific linguistic and rhetorical conventions used to relay this knowledge; for example, philosophers "argue" while engineers "report" (Hyland, 2004b, p. 27).

Emotional Strengths: Beyond merely observing a candidate's friendliness and social etiquette, some LOR writers choose to comment on the inner fortitude exhibited by the individual they are recommending. While not intended to serve as a psychological evaluation, these written descriptions highlight the character qualities describing an applicant's affective domain (e.g., bravery, persistence, integrity, and vitality).

Emphasizers: Stance-based features that add a forceful sense to syntax.

Engagement: An alignment dimension where writers acknowledge and connect to others, recognizing the presence of their readers, pulling them along with their argument, focusing their attention, acknowledging their uncertainties, including them as discourse participants, and guiding them to interpretations (Hyland, 2001).

English for Specific Purposes (ESP): An approach to language instruction that prepares users to communicate at a professional level in a specific profession. An ESP course will focus on one a particular field (e.g., business English, scientific English, aviation English) and emphasize the specific vocabulary and skills learners need to be competent users of the language of this field.

English for Academic Purposes (EAP): This approach is one of the most common forms of ESP. The instruction mainly focuses on developing the linguistic skills and mastering the conventions of English in an academic context. It aims to enable international and L2 (second-language English speakers) students to attain the proficiency level of English fluency that can enable them to conduct research and complete advanced degrees in a university setting.

Epideictic Rhetoric: Hailing from ancient Greek rhetoric, epideictic rhetoric was first used in ceremonial orations to praise a fallen war hero or to blame an interlocutor. This type of laudatory rhetoric focuses on the present-tense evaluation of an individual's merit, as in a character reference. Other contemporary examples include a eulogy or a celebrity roast.

Epistemic Markers: Linguistic means by which rhetors signal the certainty or credence of their propositions. Hedging terms (e.g., "possibly," "generally," or "likely") and the eight central modals ("will," "would," "may," "might," "can," "could," "should," and "must") suggest a carefully constructed air of scholarly objectivity, whereas boosters (e.g., "find," "show," or "demonstrate") may indicate confidence in a given rhetorical position.

Evidentials/Evidentiality: A language resource that indicates the nature of evidence and information source for a given statement. An evidential, then, is the particular grammatical or lexical element (e.g., adverbials such as "apparently," "obviously," etc., or phrases such as "it seems to me") that indicates evidentiality.

Exigence: A sense of controversy or urgency compelling someone to speak or write on an issue. This lexical term signals that something controversial has occurred or is present and that a problem needs to be solved. Something is wrong, imperfect, defective, or in conflict. The urgency compelling a rhetor to speak or act adds exigence to a message. Knowing that a fellowship or graduate program is competitive or that a faculty search pits qualified applicants against each other as they vie for a single position, the exigence might be the short time frame in which to select the most suitable candidate(s).

Formulaicity: Vijay Kumar Bhatia (2004) posited that writers rely on prefabricated or conventional, formulaic phrases when communicating, instead of coming up with new ones.

Genre Analysis: Parsing a given text to see how it fits the conventions of a written category of similar text types composed for a particular communicative purpose.

Hedges: Lexical units that attempt to render a phrase more ambiguous, less certain, or improbable. In other words, they are markers (e.g., "probably," "possibly") writers use to convey less assurance.

Intellectual Strengths: Academic job and program candidates are expected to be bright, but intellectual competencies extend beyond high IQ or standardized test scores. These strengths comprise character qualities describing an applicant's intelligence (e.g., creativity, curiosity, open-mindedness, love of learning, and perspective).

Intertextuality: A loose term coined by critic Julia Kristeva in the 1960s as a general reference to how some texts feature examples or traces of other texts through allusion, quotation, pastiche, etc., to bolster verisimilitude. Intertextuality is intrinsic to any text, even if the references to other texts are not deliberate or intentional (Allen, 2000).

Kairos: The exigency or rhetorical notion of the critical moment that combines timeliness and appropriateness in constructing an appeal for a candidate's work (Bekins et al., 2004).

Letter of Recommendation (LOR): A document written on behalf of another individual up for consideration for a job opening or a spot in a competitive admissions program. It usually extols the merits of the candidate rather than listing deficiencies.

Mitigation Strategies: Strategies that people adopt to avoid face-threatening situations in interactions and thereby linguistically to repair the damage done to someone's "face" by what one says or does (Ali & Salih, 2020). In other words, these strategies are linguistic and pragmatic means by which speakers attempt to reduce harm caused by miscommunication by hedging and/or repairing damage done to one's reputation. Using indirect speech or softening one's statement to diminish the painful impact of an illocutionary act stand as examples.

Move-Step Analysis: First theorized by scholar John Swales, this method for identifying rhetorical moves and subordinated steps helped to differentiate genre analysis. Later theorists have added nuances to this approach, comparing highly specialized generic subtypes for common features—often using very large corpora collected from academic writing samples.

Narrative Episodes: When LOR writers include micro (or extended) stories as illustrations for a claim being made about a given candidate.

Occluded Genres: Genres that are "out of sight to outsiders and apprentices"—text types such as letters of recommendation and job application statements (see Swales, 2004). These text types are often hidden from public purview since they are submitted confidentially.

Positioning: The authorial "position" applicants establish for themselves in their narratives. It is a metaphorical concept that refers to clusters of beliefs that individuals may display in negotiating their roles in relation to both the issues discussed in the text and to others who hold points of view on those issues.

Promotional Discourse/Genres: Higher education requires proficiency in producing text types that burnish the credentials of oneself or others through a certain way of writing, using similar yet distinctive features depending on the rhetorical situation.

Relational Strengths: Aptitudes of an applicant that translate into positive interpersonal interactions. The character qualities of love, kindness, collegiality, and social intelligence as indicated in a letter of recommendation (LOR) wherein the writer comments on the applicant's collegiality and/or ease interacting with students.

Semantic Prosody: When certain words occur along with other words (what linguists call "collocations"), they can acquire positive or negative connotations depending on the word order. Some words often appear in tandem with others, contributing to meaning or perception of a phrase or sentence, varying by what they modify. An example given by Dominic Stewart (2010, pp. 1–3) to illustrate prosody is the phrase "break out," which may occasionally seem positive (e.g., "she was a breakout star in the 1990s") while being primarily perceived negatively (e.g., "a COVID-19 breakout" or "the war had broken out").

Stance: Related to positioning, this concept can refer to either how authors position themselves relative to their own texts or the persuasive position of the rhetor in relation to the audience, whether tentative or supportive, expert or novice, etc. This interpersonal stance is shaped by the communicative goals of the participants in any given interaction.

Support Genres: Academia—like other professional fields—hosts a number of attendant text types that help discourse participants communicate effectively. These genres require some training to learn fluency in producing them.

References ───────────────────────────────────────

Aamodt, M., & Bryan, D. (1993). Predicting performance with letters of recommendation. *Public Personnel Management, 22*(1), 81.

Aamodt, M. G., Bryan, D. A., & Whitcomb, A. J. (1989). *Validation of the Peres and Garcia technique for predicting performance with letters of recommendation.* Proceedings of the Annual Meeting of the International Personnel Management Association Assessment Council, 1989, Orlando, Florida.

Afful, J. B. A., & Kyei, E. (2020). Move analysis of letters of recommendation written by lecturers in a Ghanaian university. *Journal of English Language Teaching and Applied Linguistics, 2,* 1–11.

Akos, P., & Kretchmar, J. (2016). Gender and ethnic bias in letters of recommendation: Considerations for school counselors. *Professional School Counseling, 20*(1), 102–113.

Albakry, M. (2022, December 5). On writing and decoding recommendation letters. *Inside Higher Ed.* https://www.insidehighered.com/advice/2022/12/06/advice-junior-faculty-writing-recommendation-letters-opinion

Albakry, M. (2015). Telling by omission: Hedging and negative evaluation in academic recommendation letters. In V. Cortes & E. Csomay (Eds.), *Corpus-based research in applied linguistics* (pp. 79–98). John Benjamins.

Ali, A. I., & Salih, S. M. (2020). Taxonomy of mitigation devices in English language. *Koya University Journal of Humanities and Social Sciences, 3*(1), 31–40.

Allen, G. (2000). *Intertextuality.* Routledge.

Antonacci, P. (2020, November 9). Reference letters in academic admissions: Useful or useless? *Acuity Insights.* https://acuityinsights.com/admissions/reference-letters-academic-admissions-useful-useless/

Aull, L. (2015). Linguistic attention in rhetorical genre studies and first-year writing. *Composition Forum, 31.* https://compositionforum.com/issue/31/linguistic-attention.php

Autry, M. K., & Carter, M. (2015). Unblocking occluded genres in graduate writing: Thesis and dissertation support services at North Carolina State University. *Composition Forum, 31*. https://compositionforum. com/issue/31/north-carolina-state.php

Bailyn, L. (2003). Academic careers and gender equity: Lessons learned from MIT. *Gender, Work & Organization, 10*(2), 137–153. https://doi. org/10.1111/1468-0432.00008

Bawarshi, A. S. (2010). Rhetorical genre studies. In A. S. Bawarshi & M. J. Reiff (Eds.), *Genre: An introduction to history, theory, research, and pedagogy* (pp. 78–104). Parlor Press.

Bazerman, C. (1988). *Shaping written knowledge: The genre and activity of the experimental article in science*. The WAC Clearinghouse.

Bekins, L. K., Huckin, T. N., & Kijak, L. (2004). The personal statement in medical school applications: Rhetorical structure in a diverse and unstable context. *Issues in Writing, 15*(1), 56–75.

Belcher, D. D., Barron Serrano, F. J., & Yang, H. S. (2016). English for professional academic purposes. In K. Hyland & P. Shaw (Eds.), *The Routledge handbook of English for academic purposes* (pp. 502–514). Routledge.

Bhatia, V. K. (2014). *Analysing genre: Language use in professional settings*. Routledge.

Bhatia, V. K. (2004). *Worlds of written discourse: A genre-based view*. Continuum.

Biber, D. (2006). *University language: A corpus-based study of spoken and written registers*. John Benjamins.

Biber, D., Connor, U., and Upton, T. A. (2007). *Discourse on the move: Using corpus analysis to describe discourse structure*. John Benjamins.

Biber, D., Johansson, S., Leech, G., Conrad, S., & Finegan, E. (1999). *Longman grammar of written and spoken English*. Longman.

Broughton, W., & Conlogue, W. (2001). What search committees want. *Profession*, 39–51.

Brown, P., & Levinson, S. (1987). *Politeness: Some universals in language usage*. Cambridge University Press.

Brown, R. M. (2004). Self-composed rhetoric in psychology personal statements. *Written Communication, 21*(3), 242–260.

Brown University. (2023). *Writing Letters of Recommendation*. https:// www.brown.edu/academics/college/fellowships/information-resources/writing-letters-recommendation/writing-letters-recommendation

Bruce, I. (2008). *Academic writing and genre: A systematic analysis.* Continuum.

Bruland, H. (2009). Rhetorical cues and cultural clues: An analysis of the recommendation letter in English studies. *Rhetoric Review, 28*(4), 406–424.

Burgess, S., & Martín-Martín, P. (Eds.). (2008). *English as an additional language in research publication and communication.* Peter Lang.

Burrough-Boenish, J. (2003). Shapers of published NNS research articles. *Journal of Second Language Writing, 12,* 223–243.

Casal, J. E., & Kessler, M. (2020). Form and rhetorical function of phrase-frames in promotional writing: A corpus- and genre-based analysis. *System, 95.* https://doi.org/10.1016/j.system.2020.102370

Chamorro-Premuzic, T., & Furnham, A. (2010). Letters of recommendation. In *The psychology of personnel selection* (pp. 52–61). Cambridge University Press.

Cheng, A. (2018). *Genre and graduate-level research writing.* University of Michigan Press.

Christie, F., & Martin, J. R. (Eds.). (2000). *Genre and institutions: Social processes in the workplace and school.* Continuum.

Colarelli, S. M., Hechanova-Alampay, R., & Canali, K. G. (2002). Letters of recommendation: An evolutionary psychological perspective. *Human Relations, 55*(3), 315–344.

Connor, U., & Upton, T. A. (Eds.). (2004). *Discourse in the professions: Perspectives from corpus linguistics.* John Benjamins.

Cotos, E., Huffman, S., & Link, S. (2020). Understanding graduate writers' interaction with and impact of the Research Writing Tutor during revision. *Journal of Writing Research, 12*(1), 187–232. https://doi.org/10.17239/jowr-2020.12.01.07

Daniel, D. (1990). Validity of a standardized reference checklist. *Applied H.R.M. Research, 1,* 51–66.

Drummond, S., & Nadworny, E. (2017, February 27). Hey, students: 5 things that are wrong with your cover letter. *NPR.*

Dutt, K., Pfaff, D. L., Bernstein, A. F., Dillard, J. S., & Block, C. J. (2016). Gender differences in recommendation letters for postdoctoral fellowships in geoscience. *Nature Geoscience, 9,* 805–808.

Ewen, R. B. (1998). *Personality: A topical approach.* Erlbaum.

Feak, C. (2009). Negotiating publication: Author's responses to peer review of medical research articles in thoracic surgery. *Revista Canaria de Estudios Ingleses, 59,* 17–34.

Feak, C., & Swales, J. M. (2011). *Creating contexts: Writing introductions across genres.* University of Michigan Press.

Feak, C., & Swales, J. M. (2009). *Telling a research story: Writing a literature review.* University of Michigan Press.

Feng, H., & Shi, L. (2004). Genre analysis of research grant proposals. *LSP & Professional Communication, 4,* 8–32.

Filippou, P., Mahajan, S., Deal, A., Wallen, E. M., Tan, H. J., Pruthi, R. S., & Smith, A. B. (2019). The presence of gender bias in letters of recommendations written for urology residency applicants. *Urology,* 134, 56–61.

Fortanet, I. (2008). Evaluative language in peer review referee reports. *Journal of English for academic purposes, 7*(1), 27–37.

The frenzied folly of professorial groupthink: A dust-up over an open letter signed by star scholars reflects a troubling trend. (2022). *The Chronicle of Higher Education, 68*(13), 48+. https://link.gale.com/apps/doc/A697720576/AONE?u=kirk10507&sid=bookmark-AONE&xid=672c9494

French, J. C., Zolin, S. J., Lampert, E., Aiello, A., Bencsath, K. P., Ritter, K. A., Strong, A. T., Lipman, J. M., Valente, M. A., & Prabhu, A. S. (2019). Gender and letters of recommendation: A linguistic comparison of the impact of gender on general surgery residency applicants. *Journal of Surgical Education, 76*(4), 899–905.

Giltrow, J. (2002). Meta-genre. In R. Coe, L. Lingard, & T. Teslenko (Eds.), *The rhetoric and ideology of genre: Strategies for stability and change* (pp. 187–205). Hampton Press.

Girzadas Jr., D. V., Harwood, R. C., Dearie, J., & Garrett, S. (1998). A comparison of standardized and narrative letters of recommendation. *Academic Emergency Medicine, 5*(11), 1101–1104.

Grice, H. P. (1975). Logic and conversation. In P. Cole and J. Morgan (Eds.), *Syntax and semantics* (vol. 3, pp. 41–58). Academic Press.

Halliday, M. A. K., & Martin, J. R. (1993). *Writing science: Literacy and discursive power.* Palmer Press.

Hargrove, J. S. (2022). Gender bias in letters of recommendation. *Fisheries, 47*(7), 289–289.

Hewings, M. (2004). An "important contribution" or "tiresome reading"? A study of evaluation in peer reviews of journal article submissions. *Journal of Applied Linguistics, 1*(3), 247–274.

Hoffman, A., Ghoubrial, R., McCormick, M., Matemavi, P., & Cusick, R. (2020). Exploring the gender gap: Letters of recommendation to pediatric surgery fellowship. *The American Journal of Surgery, 219*(6), 932–936.

Hogan, R. (2005). In defense of personality measurement: New wine for old whiners. *Human Performance, 18*(4), 331–341.

Hunston, S. (2007). Semantic prosody revisited. *International Journal of Corpus Linguistics, 12*(2), 249–268.

Hunston, S., & Thompson, G. (Eds.). (1999). *Evaluation in text.* Oxford University Press.

Hunter, J. C. (2004). *The world's most powerful leadership principle: How to become a servant leader.* Crown Business.

Hyland, K. (2004a). A convincing argument: Corpus analysis and academic persuasion. In U. Connor & T. A. Upton (Eds.), *Discourse in the professions: Perspectives from corpus linguistics* (pp. 87–112). John Benjamins.

Hyland, K. (2001). Bringing in the reader: Addressee features in academic writing. *Written Communication, 18*, 549–574.

Hyland, K. (2004b). *Disciplinary discourses, Michigan classics ed.: Social interactions in academic writing.* University of Michigan Press.

Hyland, K. (2003). Dissertation acknowledgements: The anatomy of a Cinderella genre. *Written Communication, 20*(3), 242–268.

Hyland, K. (2004c). *Genre and second language writing.* University of Michigan Press.

Hyland, K. (1998). *Hedging in scientific research articles.* John Benjamins.

Hyland, K. (2012). Individuality or conformity? Identity in personal and university academic homepages. *Computers and Composition, 29*(4), 309–322. https://doi.org/10.1016/j.compcom.2012.10.002

Hyland, K., & Diani, G. (Eds.). (2009). *Academic evaluation: Review genres in university settings.* Springer.

Hyon, S. (2008). Convention and inventiveness in an occluded academic genre: A case study of retention-promotion-tenure reports. *English for Specific Purposes, 27*(2), 175–192.

Hyon, S. (1996). Genre in three traditions: Implications for ESL. *TESOL Quarterly, 30*(4), 693–722.

Isaac, C., Chertoff, J., Lee, B., & Carnes, M. (2011). Do students' and authors' genders affect evaluations? A linguistic analysis of medical student performance evaluations. *Academic Medicine, 86*(1), 59–66. https://doi.org/10.1097/ACM.0b013e318200561d

Knouse, S. B. (1983). The letter of recommendation: Specificity and favorability of information. *Personnel Psychology, 36,* 331–341.

Liberman, M. (2010, January 5). Lying by telling the truth? *Language Log.* https://languagelog.ldc.upenn.edu/nll/?p=2023

Liberman, M. (2012, April 24). The quality of quantity. *Language Log.* https://languagelog.ldc.upenn.edu/nll/?p=3922

Lopez, S., Oehlert, M., & Moberly, R. (1996). Selection criteria for American Psychological Association-accredited internship programs: A survey of training directors. *Professional Psychology: Research and Practice, 27*(5), 518–520.

Lorés, R. (2004). On RA abstracts: From rhetorical structure to thematic organization. *English for Specific Purposes, 23,* 208–302.

Loudermilk, B. C. (2007). Occluded academic genres: An analysis of the MBA thought essay. *Journal of English for Academic Purposes*, *6*(3), 190–205.

Lu, X., Yoon, J., Kisselev, O., Casal, J. E., Liu, Y., Deng, J., & Nie, R. (2021). Rhetorical and phraseological features of research article introductions: Variation among five social science disciplines. *System, 100,* 102543. https://doi.org/10.1016/j.system.2021.102543

MacRae, P. (2019). *Business and professional writing: A basic guide* (2nd ed.). Broadview Press.

Madera, J. M., Hebl, M. R., & Martin, R. C. (2009). Gender and letters of recommendation for academia: Agentic and communal differences. *Journal of Applied Psychology, 94*(6), 1591.

Madera, J. M., Hebl, M. R., Dial, H., Martin, R., & Valian, V. (2019). Raising doubt in letters of recommendation for academia: Gender differences and their impact. *Journal of Business and Psychology, 34,* 287–303.

Martin, J., & White, P. (2005). *The language of evaluation: Appraisal in English*. Palgrave Macmillan.

Matsuda, P. K., & Tardy, C. M. (2007). Voice in academic writing: The rhetorical construction of author identity in blind manuscript review. *English for Specific Purposes,* 26(2), 235–249.

McCarthy, J. M., & Goffin, R. D. (2001). Improving the validity of letters of recommendation: An investigation of three standardized reference forms. *Military Psychology, 13,* 199–222. https://doi.org/10.1207/S15327876MP1304_2

Mehrabian, A. (1965). Communication length as an index of communicator attitude. *Psychological Reports, 17*(2), 519–522.

Merkel, W. (2020). "What I mean is . . .": The role of dialogic interactions in developing a statement of teaching philosophy. *Journal of Second Language Writing, 48*(100702), 1–12.

Miller, C. M. (1984). Genre as social action. *Quarterly Journal of Speech, 70*(2), 151–167.

Miller, R., & Van Rybroek, G. (1988). Internship letters of recommendation: Where are the other 90%? *Professional Psychology: Research and Practice, 19*(1), 115–117.

Nattinger, J. R., & DeCarrico, J. S. (1992). *Lexical phrases and language teaching.* Oxford University Press.

Neaderhiser, S. E. (2016a). Conceiving of a teacherly identity: Metaphors of composition in teaching statements. *Pedagogy, 16*, 413–443.

Neaderhiser, S. E. (2016b). Hidden in plain sight: Occlusion in pedagogical genres. *Composition Forum, 33*, 1–14.

Nicklin, J. M., & Roch, S. G. (2009). Letters of recommendation: Controversy and consensus from expert perspectives. *International Journal of Selection & Assessment, 17*(1), 76–91.

Omidian, T., Shahriari, H., & Siyanova-Chanturia, A. (2018). A cross-disciplinary investigation of multi-word expressions in the moves of research article abstracts. *Journal of English for Academic Purposes, 36*, 1–14.

Paltridge, B. (2002). Thesis and dissertation writing: An examination of published advice and actual practice. *English for Specific Purposes, 21*, 125–143.

Peres, S. H., & Garcia, J. R. (1962). Validity and dimensions of descriptive adjectives used in reference letters for engineering applicants. *Personnel Psychology, 15*(3), 279–286.

Peterson, C., & Seligman, M. E. P. (2004). *Character strengths and virtues: A handbook and classification.* Oxford University Press.

Rauen, F. J. (2009). Relevance and genre: Theoretical and conceptual interfaces. In C. Bazerman, A. Bonini, & D. Figueiredo (Eds.), *Genre in a changing world* (pp. 57–77). WAC Clearinghouse.

Rief, L. (2019). What's next in writing must be what was in writing. *Voices from the Middle, 26*(4), 31–34. https://www.proquest.com/scholarly-journals/whats-next-writing-must-be-what-was/docview/2279758036/se-2

Rowley-Jolivet, E., & Carter-Thomas, S. (2005). Genre awareness and rhetorical appropriacy: Manipulation of information structure by NS and NNS scientists in the international conference setting. *English for Specific Purposes, 24*, 41–64.

Ryan, M., & Martinson, D. (2000). Perceived effects of exaggeration in recommendation letters. *Journalism & Mass Communication Educator, 55*(1), 40–52.

Samraj, B. (2014). Move structure. In K. P. Schneider & A. Barron (Eds.), *Pragmatics of discourse* (pp. 385–406). DeGruyter Mouton.

Samraj, B., & Monk, L. (2008). The statement of purpose in graduate program applications: Genre structure and disciplinary variation. *English for Specific Purposes, 27*(2), 193–211.

Sarraf, D., Vasiliu, V., Imberman, B., & Lindeman, B. (2021). Use of artificial intelligence for gender bias analysis in letters of recommendation for general surgery residency candidates. *The American Journal of Surgery, 222*(6), 1051–1059.

Schmader, T., Whitehead, J., & Wysocki, V. (2007). A linguistic comparison of letters of recommendation for male and female chemistry and biochemistry job applicants. *Sex Roles, 57*(7–8), 509–514.

Schumacher, J. (2015). *Dear committee members: A novel.* Anchor.

Shaw, P., Kuteeva, M., & Okamura, A. (2014). Submission letters for academic publication: Disciplinary differences and promotional language. *Journal of English for Academic Purposes, 14*, 106–117.

Soler-Monreak, C. (2015). Announcing one's work in PhD theses in computer science: A comparison of move 3 in literature reviews written in English L1, English L2 and Spanish L1. *English for Specific Purposes, 40*, 27–41.

Stewart, D. (2010). *Semantic prosody: A critical introduction.* Routledge.

Swales, J. M. (1981). *Aspects of article introductions.* Language Studies Unit, University of Aston.

Swales, J. M. (1990). *Genre analysis: English in academic and research settings.* Cambridge University Press.

Swales, J. M. (1996). Occluded genres in the academy: The case of the submission letter. In E. Ventola & A. Mauranen (Eds.), *Academic writing: Intercultural and textual issues* (pp. 45–58). John Benjamins.

Swales, J. M. (2004). *Research genres: Explorations and applications.* Cambridge University Press.

Swales, J. M., & Feak, C. (2009). *Abstracts and the writing of abstracts.* University of Michigan Press.

Swales, J. M., & Feak, C. (2012). *Commentary for academic writing for graduate students, 3rd ed.: Essential tasks and skills.* University of Michigan Press.

Swales, J. M., & Feak, C. (2011). *Navigating academia: Writing supporting genres.* University of Michigan Press.

Swangboonsatic, C. (2006): *Text and context in international trade communication: A case study of e-mail: Business communication among professionals in the Asia-Pacific region* [Doctoral dissertation, Victoria University of Technology, Melbourne].

Tardy, C. M. (2016). *Beyond convention: Genre innovation in academic writing.* University of Michigan Press.

Tardy, C., & Swales, J. (2014). Genre analysis. In K. P. Schneider & A. Barron (Eds.), *Pragmatics of discourse* (pp. 165–187). DeGruyter Mouton.

Tomlinson, E., & Newman, S. (2018). Epideictic rhetoric born digital: Evolution of the letter of recommendation genre. *Journal of Business and Technical Communication, 32*(1), 3–37.

Trix, F., & Psenka, C. (2003). Exploring the color of glass: Letters of recommendation for female and male medical faculty. *Discourse & Society, 14*(2), 191–220.

Turrentine, F. E., Dreisbach, C. N., St Ivany, A. R., Hanks, J. B., & Schroen, A. T. (2019). Influence of gender on surgical residency applicants' recommendation letters. *Journal of the American College of Surgeons, 228*(4), 356–365.

Upton, T. A., & Cohen, M. A. (2009). An approach to corpus-based discourse analysis: The move analysis as example. *Discourse Studies, 11*(5), 585–605.

Wang, H. S., & Flowerdew, J. (2016). Participatory genre analysis of statements of purpose: An identity-focused study. *Writing and Pedagogy, 8*(1), 65–89.

Yakhontova, T. (2013). "Selling" or "telling"? The issue of cultural variation in research genres. In J. Flowerdew (Ed.), *Academic discourse* (pp. 216–232). Routledge.

Yang, W. (2015). "Call for papers": Analysis of the schematic structure and lexico-grammar of CFPs for academic conferences. *English for Specific Purposes, 37*(1), 39–51.

Yates, J., & Orlikowski, W. (1992). Genres of organizational communication: A structural approach to studying communication and media. *Academy of Management Review, 17*(2), 299–326.

Index